11/99

 St. Louis Community College

Forest Park
Florissant Valley
Meramec

Instructional Resources
St. Louis, Missouri

Sixties Rock

Music in American Life

A list of books in the series appears at the end of this book.

Sixties Rock

Garage, Psychedelic, and Other Satisfactions

Michael Hicks

University of Illinois Press

Urbana and Chicago

Publication of this book was supported by a grant from the
Sonneck Society for American Music.

This book is printed on acid-free paper.

Library of Congress Cataloging-in-Publication Data
Hicks, Michael, 1956–
Sixties rock: garage, psychedelic, and other satisfactions /
Michael Hicks.
p.   cm. — (Music in American life)
Includes bibliographical references (p.   ) and index.
ISBN 0-252-02427-3 (cloth: acid-free paper)
1. Rock music—United States—1961–1970—History and criticism.
I. Title.
II. Series.
ML3534.H53   1999
781.66—ddc21   98-8992
CIP
MN

Contents

Illustrations follow page 74

Preface

"Rock" is a weighty, confusing, indispensable, and often irrelevant term. Consider, for example, that most people use the term "rock" when referring to the youth-oriented popular music of the 1960s. Yet, in doing so they actually refer to a dazzling profusion of styles. Rock of the 1960s includes the music of artists as diverse as the Beach Boys, Otis Redding, Simon and Garfunkel, and Led Zeppelin. How useful could any term be that embraces all their styles? Fortunately, most listeners now use specialized terms to describe the subcategories of rock. Those listeners might describe the music of the foregoing artists as, respectively, surf music, soul music, folk rock, and early heavy metal (although some would disagree on even those terms). But the persistent and ubiquitous use of the word "rock" constantly provokes attempts to define it.[1]

For many listeners "rock" differs considerably from "rock 'n' roll." If one listens carefully to the recorded legacy of the 1950s and 1960s, one senses that the dance/romance-based music known as rock 'n' roll evolved into something more ambitious in its aesthetic content. Rock musicians played music that was, as the slang of the 1960s proclaimed it, "heavy"— not necessarily in its aural substance (which in any case is difficult to weigh) but in its intentions and aspirations. Unlike their rock 'n' roll predecessors, many rock artists of the mid-1960s came to consider themselves precisely that: they were *artists,* self-conscious makers of a new sonic medium. Before that time, as Charles Hamm suggests, rock 'n' roll could not be separated from "the loose collection of styles comprising the post–Tin Pan Alley repertory," what most people refer to as "pop" music.[2] Rock artists tried to distance themselves from pop, in search of an art medium possessing all the cultural durability that, indeed, the word "rock" implies.

Sixties Rock is a mosaic about some facets of that art medium. The book purports to be neither a comprehensive history of rock during that period, nor a taxonomy of its styles and subcategories, nor a polemic about its self-evident joys. Some of the major artists who shaped rock in the 1960s fail to appear in *Sixties Rock*—not only those mentioned above (the Beach Boys et al.) but also looming figures like Bob Dylan, clearly one of the most important musicians of recent decades. Even the Beatles hardly appear until chapter seven, where, for reasons that will become clear, they suddenly dominate. Dylan and the Beatles, of course, are usually considered fountainheads of rock; indeed, Robert Christgau defined rock as "all music derived primarily from the energy and influence of the Beatles—and maybe Bob Dylan, and maybe you should stick pretensions in there someplace."[3] The Beatles and Dylan, who obviously cannot suffer from any neglect here, receive abundant attention elsewhere. But the music with which we deal here seems best viewed through lenses relatively free from the powerful spectres of the Beatles and Dylan. As the subtitle explains, this book focuses on the garage-psychedelic nexus in sixties rock.

Garage rock and psychedelic music contain both the whiff of trivia and the stuff of greatness. Like the low-budget exploitation movies of the same era, these rock styles permeated American culture, furnishing it with blatant, often naive musical gestures. But garage rock and psychedelic music also proved to be stimuli for some of the (seemingly) headier styles of the 1970s and 1980s—heavy metal, progressive rock, punk, new wave, grunge, and several hybrid forms as yet unclassifiable. Perhaps more important than their influence, garage rock and psychedelic music achieved a certain single-minded artistry that could be serious, intense, and occasionally brilliant.

Sixties Rock is primarily a collection of seven interrelated essays that, taken together, form an angular portrait of the music. In it, I begin by studying the sonic foundations of the music: "distorted" voices and guitars. How did the superficially coarse singing actually enliven the music? And why did electric guitarists try to make their equipment sound as if it were broken? I go on to study the adjectives "garage" and "psychedelic." Many writers use "garage" as a modifier of the term "rock," as though some tangible musical traits combined in "garage rock" to make a uniform style. Probably so. But what are those traits (and what do they have to do with the word "garage")? Many writers also use the adjective "psychedelic" as though the ties between the drugs and the music were obvious. But what, precisely, are those ties?

Many rock songs from this period deserve close attention. After exploring garage rock I devote a full chapter to one of the most popular songs in the garage repertoire: "Hey Joe." Why this song (indeed, this international phenomenon) deserves a whole chapter will, I hope, become clear. After discussing psychedelic music I give a chapter to one of the most celebrated psychedelic songs, the Doors' "Light My Fire"—a song that the Doors constantly tried to reshape in ways (and for reasons) detailed in that chapter.

In the late 1960s many rock artists devised unusual endings for their songs. These new endings were often the quirkiest and most astonishing parts of the music. In the last chapter of this book I examine the different types of new endings, their origins, their structure, and their meaning.

In considering the foregoing topics, I always try to keep in mind the basic question: what makes the *sound* of the music so alluring?[4] This book does not provide (or attempt) a "definitive" answer. But it does suggest some new terms for describing the music's details. It also tries to rectify a certain fuzziness about terms already in use. Conventional terminology, as Richard Middleton so nicely puts it, is a sieve, catching and holding some things and "letting anything foreign to its sphere of competence escape."[5] In the quest to capture the things that escape the terminological sieve one can either invent new jargon or create metaphors. New jargon makes for a finer sieve; metaphors transcend the filtering process in hopes of holistic comprehension. Each approach has its advantages and liabilities. In *Sixties Rock* I try both, following my intuition about when to tighten the sieve and when to discard it.

Sixties Rock aspires to clarity through a methodology that is not always so clear. The means to understanding rock are as eclectic as the music itself (see appendix 1). Each chapter uses whatever tools and angles of vision seem best to see and grasp its subject. Each topic summons different responses to its complexities. While the book focuses on a relatively small body of music in a short space of time, it makes connections across styles and decades in a somewhat freewheeling way. Thus one will find connections among artists and styles as diverse as: jazz trumpeters of the 1920s, the Everly Brothers, British folk music, Latin dance beats, Karlheinz Stockhausen, popular "standards," Indian music, Hank Williams, West African dance music, and Bach. If this list seems perplexing at first glance, it will become clear as the book proceeds.

*

Writing this book was harder but more rewarding than any writing I have done. The sources were far flung, often ephemeral. The potential audience was broad and diverse. The repertoire was elusive—almost every week that I was writing, some old record caught my ear and pushed its way into my conception of the music. Other, safer projects (with real deadlines) kept interrupting this one. The book never quite seemed finished. But I hope it now seems ripe for reading.

For bringing it to this point I must mention many people, with pre-emptive apologies to those whose names I may have ungraciously (but not intentionally) omitted. The staff at *Discoveries* magazine generously print-ed my call for versions of "Hey Joe"; a few readers responded to the call in especially helpful ways: Charles Fontaine, Jeff Lemlich, Bjorn Luka, Mike Markesich, Jim Oldsberg, Bruce Partridge, Jeff Riedle, David Schumann, Neal Skok, Joe Tortelli, and Dave Tulloch. The chapter on "Light My Fire" could not have come about without the learned advice and assistance of the proprietor of the Doors Collectors Club, Kerry Humpherys. Several people gave substantial historical information over the phone—they are cited in the chapter notes. Countless other people loaned me books, pho-tocopied articles, dubbed records, and pointed me in directions I had not foreseen. Some people read drafts of the whole manuscript and offered encouragement and advice: John Covach, Thomas Durham, Charles Hamm, Brian Harker, Stephan Lindeman, Doug Martin, Craig Russell, Kim Simpson, Neal Skok, and Robert Walser. Innumerable colleagues and stu-dents read chapter drafts, heard me read papers, discussed the concepts with me, and offered astute criticism. Foremost among these colleagues is Steven Johnson. From this book's inception he has discussed every fac-et of the work with me, read several drafts of every chapter, and promot-ed my work to fellow scholars. Judy McCulloh, Margo Cheney, and oth-ers at the University of Illinois Press eagerly and patiently nurtured this work to its final form. Finally, I must thank my wife, Pam, daughters Ra-chel and Julia, and sons Caleb and John for being tolerant as month after month I brought home boxes full of records, tapes, and compact discs, cranked up the volume, and scribbled.

Sixties Rock

1 The Against-the-Grain of the Voice

Mick Jagger remarked in 1968, "I can't hardly sing, you know what I mean?"[1] Many who heard him agreed. A typical critique of the Rolling Stones' lead singer claims that he "seems to have about five good notes. All the rest come out shouted, squawked, or slurred to the point that the melodies he sings—and they are damned simple melodies, at that—are often altogether lost. . . . he hardly manages to keep the tunes afloat."[2] An otherwise admiring biographer describes Jagger's voice as "unexceptional" and quotes a former member of the Rolling Stones as calling that voice "thin" and "off-key."[3]

Why, then, is Jagger one of the most influential singers of his generation? The answer lies partly in what is nowadays called the "grain of the voice," his unique vocal sonority (an aesthetic category introduced by Roland Barthes).[4] Another way to look at Jagger's influence, however, is to consider what could be called the "against-the-grain" of his voice, that is, his special knack for vocal self-contradiction.[5] The vocal self-contradiction of which I speak has two parts. The first and most elemental is physiological: the singer uses techniques that make the voice seem to be fighting against itself, obstructing tone at the same time as it is producing it. The second part of self-contradiction is psychological: the singer uses techniques that complicate his persona, implying two or more identities behind the singing. Physiological self-contradiction gives dramatic intensity and shape; psychological self-contradiction creates a cast of characters. Both kinds of self-contradiction flow from an idea of singing nicely expressed by Simon Frith: "Songs are more like plays than poems."[6] Which is to say, songs depend more on conflict and characterization than on imagery and sonority. Mick Jagger keenly demonstrated how one can refract one's voice into competing "voices."

To take inventory of some techniques that generate self-contradiction we will require some new terms, though not a strict technical jargon. The terms we will use are not "scientific," but they do derive from a real vocal taxonomy, a set of categories that one can hear in Mick Jagger's singing, in those who foreshadowed and emulated him, and in those who furthered his process of vocal self-contradiction.[7]

*

Two common, fundamental forms of physiological self-contradiction appear in most rock singing. Both derive from African-American styles, one directly, the other indirectly.[8] The first form of self-contradiction we may call the "roar," the guttural belt style of singing in which the singer opposes laryngeal and pharyngeal forces to create a gravelly, gurgling sonority. The technique has roots in revivalist preaching and gospel singing; one can hear it powerfully displayed in recordings such as those by Blind Willie Johnson and Reverend Johnny Blakey in the 1920s. By the 1950s many rhythm and blues artists adopted this sort of continuous roar—Roy Byrd (a.k.a. Professor Longhair), Louis Jordan, Edgar Blanchard, Screamin' Jay Hawkins, Little Richard, and, occasionally, Ray Charles (e.g., in "Mess Around," 1953). In many of these recordings, the roar intertwines with the overall musical fabric, which seemed obsessed with rapid fibrillations of many kinds, from piano tremolos to electronic echo effects.

A singer could also use the roar selectively, to enhance the song's textual rhetoric and reinforce its most emphatic points. Blues singers such as Muddy Waters, B. B. King, and Bobby Bland tended to use the roar in this way, as one of a catalogue of vocal devices aimed at intensifying selected words. Waters, for example, employs a roar almost exclusively on the word "I" in his 1954 recording of Willie Dixon's "I Just Want to Make Love to You," emphasizing the self-centered machismo of the text. Ray Charles uses the roar similarly in "Early in the Morning" (1960), employing it only on the exclamations of "I know" in the choruses. Most early rock 'n' roll singers roared only in this rhetorical way, as a form of textual accent rather than a timbral/articulative norm. The Coasters' recording of "Searchin'" (1957), however, gives a good example of the rhetorical roar linked to a large-scale design. In the first verse, lead singer Billy Guy roars sparingly, usually on the word "searchin.'" He roars more frequently in successive verses until it becomes nearly continuous. But by the last verse, he has also transformed the roar into what we may call a "buzz."

Unlike the roar, the buzz comes from the upper part of the throat and the nasal cavity, producing a grinding, raspy sound. Where the roar is guttural and oscillates with discrete, more differentiated pulsations (like a combustion engine) the higher-pitched buzz oscillates far more rapidly (like an electric motor). Many aspiring white rock 'n' roll singers preferred the buzz to the roar, probably because it was easier to produce and less painful to the throat. Like the roar, the buzz came in continuous and discontinuous versions. Sun recording artist Billy Riley sings with a continuous Popeye-like buzz in novelty recordings such as "Flying Saucers Rock and Roll" and "Red Hot" (both 1957, the latter apparently derived from Robert Johnson's early buzzing on "They're Red Hot," 1936). Eddie Cochran sings similarly in some of his early recordings, such as "Let's Get Together" (later remade, and somewhat differently sung by him as "C'mon Everybody," 1958). Discontinuous versions of the buzz ranged from Cochran's selective use of it in "Summertime Blues" (1958)—e.g., on "I'm a gonna" in the choruses—to Elvis Presley's buzz on the single word "there's" in the first line of the first verse of "Good Rockin' Tonight" (1954).

Both the roar and the buzz sounded like vocal isometrics, aural images of opposing forces producing friction. Both well suited primal expressions of lust or rage; both connoted virility, as if the singer were lifting weights. In that spirit, many rock singers of the mid-to-late-1960s used the roar and the buzz as rock 'n' roll singers had in earlier years. Rick Derringer of the McCoys buzzes in "Hang On Sloopy" (1965), as does Tommy James (of the Shondells) in "Mony Mony" (1968). Throughout her short-lived fame (1967–70), Janis Joplin buzzed with extraordinary intensity. Among British singers, Eric Burdon preferred the roar—hear his cover (1964) of Berry's smooth-voiced "Around and Around"—while Van Morrison (of Them) preferred the buzz (almost continuous in "Gloria," but only on the words "well here it comes" in "Here Comes the Night," both from 1965). Less successfully, some fragile-voiced singers occasionally attempted to use these techniques. Both Gerry Roslie of the Sonics and Rich Brown of the Wilde Knights attempt continuous rhythm and blues-style roars in many of their recordings of the early- to mid-1960s. But since their voices seem unable to sustain a roar, they occasionally abandon it, with no evident rhetorical purpose.

In the late 1950s Buddy Holly developed a technique that allowed weaker singers to vary their vocal expression. That technique is what one writer calls "baby talk,"[9] a soft, high-pitched, crisply enunciated, frontally resonant singsong—a kind of nasal cooing.[10] Perhaps adapting the prattle of certain novelty recordings of the 1940s, Holly uses baby talk in the bridge of "Oh Boy!" (1957)—"you can hear my heart a-callin'"—to counterbalance his almost continuous roar and buzz in the verses. His baby talk in "Peggy Sue" (1958), especially on the fourth-verse line "I love you / Peggy Sue / with a love so rare and true," is particularly striking. Its fragility utterly contradicts the dark, incessant tom-toms underneath it. Holly's baby talk suggested anti-macho, a foil to the aggression of the roar. But Holly's frequent juxtaposition of roar and baby talk within the same song created ambivalence: which, if either of them, reflected the "real" persona of the singer? Neither dominated the other, leaving the question disturbingly unresolved.

Some pop singers copied Holly's baby talk outright (e.g., Tommy Roe in "Sheila," 1962). Some rock singers did as well, especially those with less powerful voices. Jack Ely's vocal on the Kingsmen's version of "Louie Louie" (1963) subtly echoes Holly's baby talk. Rudy Martinez frequently does the same, as in the ? [Question Mark] and the Mysterians hit "96 Tears" (1966). And the Wilde Knights' alternate lead singer (Rick Dey), used a bland, precisely declaimed baby talk in their original version of "Just Like Me" (later covered by Paul Revere and the Raiders). While many singers alternated roar/buzz and baby talk techniques from song to song, few tried to recreate Holly's stylistic tension within a single song.

One notable exception is Mark Lindsay, the lead vocalist and front man for Paul Revere and the Raiders. Lindsay demonstrated throughout his career that he was quite capable of a deep, sustained roar (notably in the introduction to "Ooo Poo Pah Doo," 1965). But in his most interesting vocals he modulates from the roar to baby talk and back. Such modulation is especially apparent in one of the Raiders' regional hits, "Over You" (1964). Throughout the song the singer threatens to kill his girl if she ever leaves him. But instead of the expected sustained roar, the singer shows his ambivalence by slipping from roar into baby talk, even in the opening lines:

┌──── Roar ────┐		┌──── Baby Talk ────┐
There's a-gonna be	some	slow, slow walkin'
There's a-gonna be	some	sad, sad talkin'

On the final words of the chorus, "if I ever hear you say we're through," Lindsay reaches a peak of pseudo-juvenile delivery. In other songs, such as "Good Thing" (1966), Lindsay moves similarly from roar (or buzz) to baby talk in the course of a single line. In the Raiders' hit cover of "Just Like Me" (1966), Lindsay departs from Rick Dey's simple baby talk: in the verses he gradually transforms close-miked baby talk into a tightly contained roar, which finally erupts full-blown in the chorus.[11] In these ways Lindsay creates some effective self-contradictions: strong vs. weak, aggressive vs. passive, dominant vs. submissive, sincere vs. sarcastic, and so forth. With such self-contradictions Lindsay—unconsciously, perhaps—exemplified what may be considered a "post-Holly" technique.

Mick Jagger took Holly's self-contradiction to a more profound level. Like many of the blues and soul singers he admired, Jagger was able to create simple, direct physiological self-contradiction in his vocalizing. Yet he also devised subtle strategies to project complexity in the absence of essential power, range, and intonational acuity. Like Holly, he juxtaposed techniques within a single song—sometimes within a single line. But his voice contradicted itself far more than Holly's in its ability to deploy layers of psychological tension.

We should note that observers differ about what Jagger's vocal ideals and models might be. Tom Wolfe describes Jagger's voice as "the voice of a bull Negro"[12] and Chris Barber claims that "Mick tries his darndest to sing like Muddy Waters and Bo Diddley."[13] Both assessments are dubious. If Jagger was imitating anyone, it was slight-voiced tenor bluesmen and rockers like Slim Harpo and Chuck Berry and country-western singers like George Jones. (Jagger, in fact, remarked: "I'm very country-influenced, from quite young—Merle Haggard, Johnny Cash, George Jones, and so on. I heard those people, really, before I heard blues.")[14] But, as David Dalton observes, Jagger's voice is "more evocative" than those British singers who emulated black vocalists because it was "personal and identifiable, instead of a facsimile."[15] Jagger always seemed to understand the limitations of his instrument and developed his voice as much as possible within its constraints. He was not gifted with an apt rhythm-and-blues voice—"I'm no Tom Jones, and I couldn't give a fuck," he once said.[16] So he developed the natural traits of his voice into a style that is part country-western and part rhythm and blues.

Like country singers, Jagger sings high notes with a nasal, straining sound. A few examples: the word "love" in the Rolling Stones' cover of Holly's "Not Fade Away" (1964) seems to resonate completely around the teeth and lips; the word "around" in "Poison Ivy" (1964) sounds, as Robert Palmer puts it, "like an amplified jew's harp";[17] on the peak notes of the chorus to "Little by Little" (1964, on the words "found out"), where one expects vibrato or some other intensification, the tone is peculiarly thin and frontal; and he delivers virtually all of Rufus Thomas's "Walking the Dog" (1964) in a whine completely alien to the roar of the original (although the harmonizing vocal features a pure buzz).

Because he lacked natural resonance, his singing is seldom free and full of the abandon one hears in rhythm and blues singers. Rather, it appears to be carefully measured in its tone and seldom flagging in its commitment to the pulse (compare Jagger's version of "Route 66" with Van Morrison's; or Jagger's "Around and Around" with Eric Burdon's). His seeming unwillingness to "cut loose" allowed Jagger to sing for hours without damaging his voice.[18] In connection with this, Jagger's concern for the health of his vocal physiology led him away from the roar and buzz, and toward his own version of baby talk. He occasionally roars, it is true, albeit with little depth, as in his cover of "I Just Want to Make Love to You" (1964); and he buzzes in his cover of the Valentinos' "It's All Over Now" (1964). But there is more than a hint of baby talk in the opening words to "Heart of Stone" (1965; "There's been so many girls that I've known"), where the technique sets up a dramatic conflict between defiant sentiment ("you'll never break this heart of stone") and boyish delivery. In "(I Can't Get No) Satisfaction" (1965) Jagger begins with a closely miked baby talk, then moves gradually further from the mike (on the words "cause I tried, and I tried, and I tried, and I tried") until he repeatedly shouts (and buzzes) on the words "I can't get no."

While rhythm and blues singers intensified selected syllables by singing louder and rougher, Jagger adapted the country-western technique of *weakening* selected syllables by singing them tentatively. He often used a kind of vocal "halt," a moment where the voice breaks, his volume drops, and the syllables seem to retreat into the throat, as though the singer were startled or suddenly vexed. In his cover of "I Just Want to Make Love to You," Jagger employs this technique at what would ordinarily be the climactic words of the bridge ("till the lights change"). Similarly, in his own "Play with Fire," Jagger's voice rises in pitch and intensity during the words "so don't play with me cause you're playing with" then suddenly weakens on the word "fire," as though the word gets caught in his throat. Such a moment connotes ambivalence, the voice doubling back on itself in order to complicate the emotional context of the phrase. As a variant of this technique, Jagger uses something we may call "disembodiment," passages where the voice inexplicably loses its passion and succumbs to a distinct dynamic flatness.[19] Jagger's detached delivery of much of "I Just Want to Make Love to You" has led to criticisms that Jagger "didn't so much sing [this song] as get it over with."[20] But here and elsewhere in Jagger's singing the strange lapses of vocal force create a conflict between the affective intent and the delivery.

The blues singers who influenced Jagger often sang with a slurred diction prompted in part by the need to obscure sexual references. The result was one of the richest aspects of their singing: a multi-layered projection of the text, in which pure sound effects compete with semantics to dominate the flow of information. Jagger tried to emulate this trait, but in a studied way. He works hard at sounding loose; in his attempts to mimic the slurred diction of old bluesmen he actually over-enunciates. He seems to give inordinate weight to the consonant "L," for instance, often letting it seep into and partially submerge the vowel that follows it. Sometimes he slurs his syllables in odd, seemingly arbitrary ways, as in his version of "Route 66" (1964) where "Oklahoma" becomes something like "onk-hama." Here and throughout his early recorded vocals Jagger exhibits a conflict between deliberate, careful diction and the slurring of the blues.

This leads to one of Jagger's most salient traits, his synthetic dialect. His "native" Cockney accent is probably exaggerated, if not affected.[21] More important, he seems to have assimilated southern American dialect in a haphazard way from blues and country recordings. From those recordings he learned to turn diphthongs into pure vowels, while at the same time turning pure vowels into diphthongs. In his versions of "Not Fade Away" and "I Just Want to Make Love to You," "I" is always "ah"; in his version of "Around and Around," "crazy sound" becomes "creezy sand" (i.e., close to Berry's original). But in these same songs "me" is "muh-ee," "bed" is "buh-ee-uhd," "shame" is "shuh-eem," and "want" is "wah-oont."

Jagger sometimes veers from song into speech. Perhaps because he struggles to sustain a single pitch without wavering, Jagger sometimes merely intones words at the end of phrases, words that would normally be sung. (In the original version of "Not Fade Away," for example, Buddy Holly sustains the last words of phrases, singing them in pitch; in his version, Jagger clips them.) He also struggles with intonation in short melodic conjunct segments (see "the place was packed" in "Around and Around"), not to mention melismas, which he generally avoids (but see the peculiar melisma on the word "away" in the fade-out to "Not Fade Away"). Amid such moments, Jagger sometimes indulges in speech-song, a blending of the two types of vocalism. Speech-song resembles the improvisatory style of certain blues and soul singers, who followed the spontaneous speech-song of black preaching. There, however, the listener senses that the performer has determined the pitch to be sung while the spoken tone is still underway; points of arrival are definite and a certain melodic coherence emerges. With Jagger's speech-song, the listener often perceives an ambivalence toward pitch, as though the pitches that emerge are *still being considered* at the time that they are being sung. Indeed, sometimes the pitch seems to yield to the spontaneous and unpredictable direction of an unbridled voice.

The early Rolling Stones song "Empty Heart" (1964) showcases Jagger's far-flung vocal devices. The harmony of the song consists entirely of a two-measure, four-chord progression (I-♭VII | IV-V), played more than forty-five times. The text contains only seven lines, each repeated two, three, or four times. Most of the lines are terse and simple-minded—e.g., "I want my love again," "Take it down," and "C'mon back to me, baby." Within the first two lines (and their repetitions), Jagger employs a halt, baby talk, speech-song, and disembodiment; moreover, he gradually dissolves the consonants of the phrase "like you wanna cry" as he repeats it. Taken together, the techniques conjure up a diverse set of conflicting attitudes—as though the "empty heart" of the singer is actually filled with competing personae.

Consider also the Stones' "Let's Spend the Night Together" (1967). Through subtle inflections Jagger turns this song into a complex psychodrama, in which lust is tempered by reticence. In the verses he vacillates between Holly-like baby talk and buzzing. But at the end of almost every line Jagger moans a plaintive "oh my my," mixing baby talk, halts, and speech-song. At the song's bridge, he shifts into an even more fragile baby talk, occasionally interrupted by a deeper voice—as though he were an adolescent undergoing a voice change (see the words "need you"—in the line "Now I *need you* more than ever"). At the line "You know I'm smilin', baby" Jagger modulates from the baby talk to a strong buzz that reaches a peak at the line "I'm just decidin', baby." His fluctuating delivery bears out that sense of "just decidin'" until the final verse, where he resolves the vocal conflicts into a consistent, hormone-driven buzz. Nevertheless, Jagger's repeats of "oh my my" increasingly sound like "oh mama"—as though the "boy" that sings so much of the text has not been subdued by the "man" who authors it.

*

Jagger established a new style of rock singing in the mid-1960s. Many singers who had cultivated their own simpler rock 'n' roll-derived vocal styles began to imitate him. Some did so quite directly in their cover versions of Rolling Stones songs: Lindsay in Paul Revere and the Raiders' "Satisfaction," Dick Peterson in the Kingsmen's "Under My Thumb," and Dick Dodd in the Standells' "Nineteenth Nervous Breakdown," to name a few. Lesser-known bands also created what may be called pseudo-covers, such as the Painted Faces' "original" song "Anxious Color" (1967), derived so unblushingly from the Stones' "Paint It, Black" (1966). But there are also hundreds of "post-Jagger" recordings, in which a lead singer transposes Jagger's vocal complexity into his own voice, creating a hybrid style of singing one generation removed from Jagger's.[22]

The most interesting "post-Jagger" singers, however, exploited the very *process* of synthesis that he had used, creating wholly new combinations and adaptations. Consider, for example, one of the most disparaged of those singers, Sky Saxon of the Seeds. Some have described Saxon as simply another American Jagger-imitator.[23] Billy Altman calls Saxon's singing "distinctly limited" (inexplicably criticizing the singer's "world view").[24] But Saxon's personal vocal synthesis is more complicated than his detractors acknowledge. In "Can't Seem to Make You Mine" (1966), the Seeds' first single, as well as in subsequent, almost identical songs (e.g., "Try to Understand," 1966), Saxon displays the components of that synthesis: he superimposes an Eddie Cochran-like buzz on classic Buddy Holly-style baby talk—replete with Holly's childlike upward portamentos (at the end of phrases). To this hybrid sonority he adds a Jagger-like pseudo-dialect, but a seemingly arbitrary one, in which vowels are colored and recolored with no particular consistency. Finally, he ornaments his lines with what we may call a "choke," a technique related to Holly's glottal stops and Jagger's halt. In the choke, the singer closes off the throat as though he were being strangled, momentarily replacing the pitched tone with a labored groan.

In some recordings, such as "Out of the Question" (1967), Saxon exaggerates his vocal pyrotechnics to gothic proportions. The rise and fall of pitch is completely unforeseeable; his speech-song, which uses far less specific pitch than even Jagger does, goes from exhilaration to pure madness. In many such situations, Saxon sings within a very narrow melodic framework, containing only three conjunct pitches (minor scale degrees: 3–2–1).[25] But he often bends the last notes of phrases in varying amounts—as much as a perfect fifth in either direction (usually up). In some songs, such as the Seeds' hit "Pushin' Too Hard" (1966), Saxon complicates the vocal melody by double-tracking it. This produces a heterophony where the two tracks ostensibly sing as one, but vary in details.[26] The heterophony may appear within a phrase, with the consonants out of synchronization; or it may appear at the end of a phrase, with the pitches of the two voices bending differently. Moreover, his chopped-up declamation of short phrases serves as a kind of counterpoint to the changing timbres of the pseudo-dialect, the occasional choke, and the heterophony.

Other post-Jagger rock singers relied heavily on a throaty, choking sound more portentous than Saxon's. Arthur Lee of the group Love, for instance (see "My Little Red Book," 1966), and Dave Aguilar of the Chocolate Watchband (see "Let's Talk about Girls," 1967) were two fine exponents of this school. Perhaps the finest, however, was Sean Bonniwell, lead singer of the Music Machine. Bonniwell superimposes aspects of Jagger's dialect and Saxon's choke onto an extremely dark tone, completely lacking in frontal resonance. (The Music Machine's instruments supported this sonority; the group tuned their guitars and bass down a half step and the drummer kept cymbals to a minimum.)[27] Unlike Jagger and Saxon, Bonniwell has unusually good intonation in long-sustained tones, yet willfully disrupts it in shorter tones. To these traits Bonniwell adds a technique borrowed from soul singing, breaking up the sustained vowel at a phrase-ending into a series of slow pulsations. Thus, at the end of the first verse of "Talk Talk" (1966), he turns "place" into "play-ay-ay-ay-ay-ay-ay-ss"; he does similarly with the word "why" at the end of each chorus to "The Eagle Never Hunts the Fly" (1968) and even the "ull" sound at the end of the word "trouble" in the first verse of "Double Yellow Line" (1968). Finally, he almost croons the sustained vowel sounds "ah" and "oh," but groans through the other vowels. All of these techniques combine to form a voice authoritative in essence and ambivalent in every detail.

Rock singing such as Jagger's, Saxon's, and Bonniwell's exploited the principle described (and condemned) in the anonymous liner notes to Julie London's album *Lonely Girl* (1955): "So many vocalists today have the annoying habit of becoming vastly different individuals when they begin to sing [and] they begin inventing a new language."[28] That unidentified author may have been referring to the rock 'n' roll singers who began the process of vocal self-contradiction. In place of conventional vocal "sincerity," they sought to instate the almost pathological ambivalence of multiple personalities. Holly and his successors (such as Mark Lindsay) simply juxtaposed macho and anti-macho forms of delivery. Jagger cultivated vast new fields of self-contradiction. He fictionalized his identity by asserting it as strong when it was weak, black when it was white, American when it was British, and even singing when it was speaking. These contradictions allowed him to infuse even his most direct statements with a sense of irony.

At the same time rock singers like Jagger created a new kind of language by pushing the words of songs through a grid of techniques like the roar, the buzz, baby talk, the halt, the choke, pseudo-dialect, and disembodiment. The new, slightly alien shapes that resulted contradicted "normal" expectations of what sung language ought to be—it was literally *contra* (i.e., against) diction. In turn, this encoding of rock words provoked a new isometrics of singing, a strenuous balancing of the forces of language and meta-language, of singing and meta-singing.

2 the Fuzz

Just as rock singers refracted their voices into multiple personalities, rock guitarists transformed their instruments into surrogate singers. Aided by new technologies, rock guitarists exchanged the instrument's historically slight musical presence (with delicate timbres, low dynamics, and rapid decay) for a new, overwhelming presence (with rough timbres, loud dynamics, and the ability to sustain—or, as Paul McCartney puts it, to "flow").[1] At the center of the exchange was a warm, powerful, sonorous sizzle known as "fuzz."

Fuzz grew inevitably from the peculiar sonic world of mid-twentieth century popular music. In the 1920s and 1930s brass players in Duke Ellington's band popularized the "growl and plunger" style of playing, a raucous mimicking of the vocal roar. By humming, flutter-tonguing, or literally growling while playing, players like Bubber Miley and Cootie Williams got tones that sounded like a controlled, distorted scream.[2] In rhythm and blues music of the 1940s and 1950s (and Motown and Memphis soul recordings of the 1960s) saxophone players routinely emulated the trumpet growls of those earlier players; by combining various hard mouthpieces and stiff reeds, by blowing with extra force, and using the techniques of Miley, Williams et al., tenor and baritone saxophone players could make the already noisy timbre of their instruments sound even more ragged.[3] Such effects allowed a player to transcend conventional virtuosity—as measured in notes per measure—in favor of a more primal, direct expression. This so-called "boot" style of tenor saxophone playing offended many purists. One complained that through it "a player of very little improvisational talent can achieve instant success with the mob by playing three or four successive choruses on one note. Provided, of course, that he heightens the impression of inspirational fervour by blowing himself blue in the face and marking time like an epileptic sergeant major."[4] Despite such cynicism, the boot style prevailed.

Although boot style began by imitating the roar and buzz of rhythm and blues singers, saxes and voices gradually achieved a symbiosis. The techniques of each reinforced the other—as Screamin' Jay Hawkins explained, his ambition was to make his voice "duplicate the sounds I got off a tenor sax."[5] But sax playing required immense physical effort, as did the roar and buzz of the singers. In all cases the sound was terse and forced, as though great strength and resistance were required to give them utterance—and they were. During the early years of rock 'n' roll, vocal and saxophonal distortion complicated the sonorous edge of the music—an edge reinforced by the sizzle of ride cymbals, snare drums, and, occasionally, maracas.

That complex of distorted sound complemented the technological basis of the rock 'n' roll industry. Most people learned rock 'n' roll through the radio, where signals competed with one another for dominance of a particular wave band. The music often came through a sieve of white noise and electrical hum that made almost any instrument or voice seem to buzz. (This was especially true of the earliest rock 'n' roll, which first appeared on some of the weakest, most remote stations.) And the records that were broadcast had their own distortion. Not only was the music typically recorded at high levels on hissing tapes, but repeated playings wore out the vinyl and made the music even fuzzier. As the predominant media of rock 'n' roll, broadcasting and recordings turned what was once an undesirable flaw into the essence of the sound. That essence signified raw power, survivability in the face of interference.

In the early twentieth century dance bands began to include guitars with brass and saxophones, a situation that created a serious imbalance of sonority: the guitar was essentially a quiet instrument, the saxophone a loud one. So in the 1920s manufacturers experimented with guitar "pickups," magnetic coils that could vibrate sympathetically with the instrument's strings. In 1931 Rickenbacker issued the first commercial electric guitar, a lap-held Hawaiian model resembling a long-handled frying pan. Later in the decade, the National and Gibson companies devised more conventionally shaped electric guitars. Meanwhile, some players began to make their own electrics by installing pickups in their acoustic (i.e., non-electric) guitars. Finally, Les Paul and Leo Fender dispensed with the guitar's resonating cavity entirely, building the first solid-body electric guitars in the late 1940s and early 1950s. With their new designs (and more refined pickups) both makers hoped to increase the instrument's tonal "purity," reducing the hum and buzz of older electrics. In the process, they redefined the electric guitar by demonstrating to the public what electrical engineers had long known: the strings of an electric guitar provoked electrical impulses directly.

Trying to keep their prices competitive, makers of electric guitar amplifiers used low-cost "P.A. grade" transformers in their equipment. At normal volume levels these transformers distorted the signal about 5 percent. But when pushed beyond their capacity—"overdriven"—the distortion levels rose to around 50 percent.[6] Black rhythm and blues guitarists usually could afford only the smallest, least powerful amps. At the same time they had to play in some of the noisiest venues. Although evidence is scarce, Robert Palmer quite plausibly suggests that bluesmen such as Muddy Waters were forced to overdrive their weak amplifiers "just to cut through the din."[7] But at some point, probably in the late 1940s, the bluesmen discovered that, by turning their amplifiers up louder than they were designed to be, they could make the guitar's timbre resemble the raunchy, distorted timbre of boot saxophone playing.

Many of the records made at Chess Studios in Chicago in the late 1940s and early 1950s captured the sound. In Howlin' Wolf's "All Night Boogie" (1953), for example, Willie Johnson's overdriven electric guitar dovetails with a similarly overdriven miked harmonica and Wolf's own "overdriven" voice to paint a perfectly consistent timbral painting. (Sun Studios in Memphis harnessed a similar sound, particularly in the guitar playing of Pat Hare.) In such cases the capturing of live distortion on records required careful engineering, since the studios wanted to faithfully document the distorted sound of the *guitars,* rather than distort the *recording* by overdriving the microphones. Whether the listener would have discerned the difference is hard to say.

Writers generally point to Guitar Slim as the electric guitarist who played the loudest, most distorted blues of the early 1950s. Playing through the P.A. system (rather than through a separate guitar amplifier), Slim always kept his guitar at maximum volume—with the club doors open to attract customers.[8] His maniacally distorted sound became legendary, not only through his performances but also through recordings like his hit "The Story of My Life" (1954), in which the guitar solo, rather than the vocal—perhaps for the first time on a rhythm and blues record—seemed the real point of the song.[9]

Like electric blues players, rock 'n' roll guitarists almost inevitably overdrove their amplifiers, trying to project their music above the sound of drums and talkative audiences. Chris Dreja of the Yardbirds assessed the situation of many groups and their early stage equipment: "God, it was basic. Between the five of us we must have had all of twenty watts. It was so quiet I could hear myself hitting the strings of my electric guitar."[10] Nevertheless, upon hearing such groups in England in 1962, Muddy Waters remarked, "Those boys were playing louder than we ever played."[11]

If overdrive was almost inevitable, some kinds of distortion were not. In many cases, accidental (and later, deliberate) damage to amplifiers enhanced the fuzzy sound. As early rock 'n' roll groups toured from club to club, the frequent moving made it likely that the cardboard cones of the speakers might be torn, or tubes damaged. In most such cases a band would simply replace the damaged part or, if times were good, buy a new amplifier. In March 1951, however, Willie Kizart tore the woofer cone of his amplifier while driving to a Jackie Brenston recording session at Sun Records in Memphis. There was neither time nor money to repair it. When the group arrived at the session with the broken speaker, producer Sam Phillips stuffed a newspaper and a sack into the hole and decided to record with the speaker as it was.[12] Tellingly, Phillips remarked, "It sounded good. It sounded like a saxophone." Phillips added that he wanted the "authentic" sound that the broken equipment gave the recording: "If they had broken-down equipment or their instruments were ragged. . . . I wanted them to go ahead and play the way they were used to playing. Because the *expression* was the thing."[13]

The result was a simple boogie record noteworthy only for the strange fuzzy sound of the guitar, which (like the saxophones in many New Orleans recordings) merely doubled the walking bass line, outlining the triads of the chord progression. Brenston and Phillips entitled it "Rocket 88," a tribute to the 1950 V-8 Oldsmobile 88, which was advertised as "the lowest priced car with 'rocket' engine."[14] While the tune was unimaginative, the novel guitar sound attracted many listeners.

Five years later, another amplifier accident reshaped the sound of Johnny Burnette's Rock 'n' Roll Trio. Guitarist Paul Burlison recalls that the strap of his Fender Deluxe amplifier broke before a show in Philadelphia, dropping the amp on the floor. "When we started playing, it sounded fuzzy, but it wasn't enough to stop the show. So Johnny looked around and grinned and we just kept on playing. When I got back to the dressing room I took the back off the amp and looked at it, and what had happened was one tube had slipped about halfway out. So I pushed the tube back up and it worked fine; pushed it back down and it'd get fuzzy."[15] Burlison's accident had not produced permanent damage, as Willie Kizart's had. Instead, the loose tube had shown him a method of tone production that was controllable (i.e., it functioned as a rheostat). It was an effect that could be switched on and off, irrespective of volume or speaker quality. In that regard, it directly foreshadowed the fuzz "controls" of the early 1960s, by which players could turn the distortion on and off with a switch.

Burlison decided to use the fuzzy guitar sound on the group's 2 July 1956 recording session for two songs, "Blues Stay Away from Me" and "Train Kept A-Rollin'." The distortion was barely noticeable in the former song, but in the latter it was prominent. As with "Rocket 88," the distorted guitar was the record's principal novelty. As "Train Kept A-Rollin'" became widely known, according to Burlison, "I had engineers calling me from all over the country asking how I got that sound."[16] Despite the interest, Burlison exploited the sound in only one subsequent recording— the calypso-based "Touch Me" (recorded March 1957).

The role of the distorted guitar in "Blues Stay Away from Me" and "Touch Me" resembled its role in "Rocket 88": it was an interesting coloration of standard guitar ostinati. It outlined the chord, provided some contrapuntal interest, and articulated the beat. But in "Train Kept A-Rollin'" Burlison uses the guitar primarily to make loud low-register plunking sounds, effectively turning it into a powerful percussion instrument. The rapid reiterations create texture and sonority for their own sake, without a conventionally functional harmonic, melodic, or bass-foundational role. Dominating the other elements of the recording, the fuzz guitar seems to emulate the chugging of a train at full speed.

Still one more accident produced another legendary distorted guitar solo. In Bobb B. Soxx and the Blue Jeans' "Zip A Dee Doo Dah" (1962), Billy Strange's electric guitar part leaked into some of the live mikes around the studio, creating a strange, growling sound. Producer Phil Spector thought it a flaw, but left it in. As engineer Larry Levine explained, Spector "didn't care what the break was gonna sound like. We played a full chorus before we got to the break, and you don't sell a song with a solo on a break."[17] But he did not envision how important a voice the lead guitar was coming to be. Described by one writer as a "tinny coil of disembodied noise," Strange's guitar break became the record's most important contribution to rock—the first Top 10 fuzz guitar solo.

In the late 1950s some electric guitarists began to damage their equipment deliberately in order to create fuzz. This happened mainly among *instrumental* rock 'n' roll bands, who continued the tradition of the rhythm and blues dance bands of the 1950s. Early rock 'n' roll instrumental bands featured saxophone, but in the late 1950s guitars took over. Without words or a lead vocalist, instrumental hits often used gimmicks and sound effects to make them memorable.

In 1958 guitarist Link Wray drove a pencil through the speaker of his amplifier before recording a new instrumental record. According to rock lore, he damaged the speaker specifically so that the guitar sound would better represent the aggressive sound of a gang brawl—a "rumble." (The truth, however, is probably that the damage came first and the record's title, "Rumble," came later. The daughter of the owner of Wray's record label said that the untitled recording reminded her of the rumble scenes in *West Side Story,* then a Broadway play. Hence the title.)[18] "Rumble" is a slow, twelve-bar (sometimes eleven-bar) blues, in which the guitar primarily plays slow, clanging chords.[19] Given its relatively innocuous harmonic and rhythmic content, "Rumble" clearly demonstrates how one could produce a Top-20 hit with little else but the sheer sonority of fuzz. Wray tried (unsuccessfully) to duplicate the success of his first fuzz record in recordings that include "Raw-Hide" (1959), "Big City after Dark" (1962), "Black Widow" (1963), and "Deuces Wild" (1964).

But Wray did inspire many guitarists of the early 1960s to follow his example. Larry Parypa of the Sonics, for instance, "was always fooling around with the amps. . . . disconnecting the speakers and poking a hole in them with an icepick."[20] Deep Purple's Ritchie Blackmore claims to have kicked in a speaker (ca. 1960) in order to create a fuzz effect.[21] Around 1963 Dave Davies of the Kinks took the 8-inch speaker of a 4-watt amplifier and "proceeded to cut [it] into ribbons with a razor blade. Then I patched it up with Sellotape and stuck a few drawing pins into it." He set this on top of his 30-watt amp, keeping the smaller one at full volume and the bigger one as low as possible.[22]

With this arrangement the Kinks produced their initial hits "You Really Got Me" and "All Day and All of the Night" (1964), which together codified the technique of "power chords"—overdriven barre chords that were given a terse, grunting quality by relaxing the left hand just enough after each strum of the right so that the ringing of the strings would be stopped. This was the guitar equivalent of the stopped articulation of raucous soul saxophone players, except that it now applied to whole harmonies.

While many guitarists wanted at least an occasional fuzz effect, few could afford to wreck their amplifiers to get it. One alternative was the recording studio: guitarists could distort their sound by recording with the input levels in the red—even if their own amplifiers sounded clean. But this still left the problem of playing fuzz in concert. The solution came from the so-called "fuzz box," a small accessory to a guitar amplifier that severely "clipped" the peaks of the instrument's natural wave form.

While most of the documentation on early fuzz boxes has been discarded or lost, the earliest such devices appear to have been introduced in 1962. The best known from that year was the Maestro Fuzztone FZ-1, a triangular brown footswitch that resembled a door stop. It allowed guitarists to control not only the tone of the instrument (i.e., treble and bass), but also the amount of distortion. Unsure of how to market such a device, the Gibson company (a distributor for Maestro) told prospective buyers that the Fuzztone would make a guitar sound like a cello![23]

The Ventures—the most popular rock 'n' roll instrumental band—probably used the Maestro device in "The 2,000 Pound Bee," parts 1 and 2, recorded in October 1962. In part 1 of this track the group plays a modified twelve-bar blues, with a single riff transposed to the level of each of the harmonies; part 2 differs only slightly. Nothing distinguishes this novelty record except for the fuzzy guitar that plays the melody. Although "2,000 Pound Bee" sold relatively poorly (only the B-side made the charts—Number 91), the Ventures continued using the fuzz box on other records. In their *Surfing with the Ventures* album (1963) they use some degree of overt distortion on nine of the twelve tracks—sometimes in accompanimental patterns, but usually in the lead melody (most prominently in the track "Barefoot Ventures"). Two subsequent singles—"Journey to the Stars" (1964) and "Pedal Pusher" (1965)—use heavy fuzz. But both failed to chart.

The "2,000 Pound Bee," however, had caught the attention of three British guitarists and a young technician who lived near them. In 1963 seventeen-year-old Roger Mayer began working for the British Admiralty as an assistant experimental officer in sound and vibration analysis. While evaluating types of distortion for his job, Mayer tried to emulate and improve upon the Ventures' fuzz guitar sounds. Making fuzz boxes soon became his hobby. He gave some of them to his friends Eric Clapton and Jimmy Page, the latter of whom passed along a fuzz box to Jeff Beck. Other guitarists also took interest in the boxes. One, Jim Sullivan, became the first to use a Mayer fuzz box on a record—P. J. Proby's minor hit "Hold Me" (1964).[24]

Jeff Beck joined the Yardbirds and used a Mayer fuzz box on one of his first recordings with the group. The three-pitch lead guitar riff of "Heart Full of Soul" (recorded February 1965) had originally been conceived for a sitar, and producer Giorgio Gomelsky hired two sitarists to play the riff at the recording session. But despite the exotic timbre, the delicacy of their sound and their rapid decay prevented the sitars from carrying the idea effectively. Beck suggested that with his fuzz box he could get an overtone-rich sound similar to that of the sitars, but with more volume and less decay. His version prevailed.[25]

The Rolling Stones forcefully brought the fuzz box to public attention in their hit "(I Can't Get No) Satisfaction." Keith Richards recalls that his own three-pitch guitar riff for the song was "actually a horn [i.e., saxophone] riff," one that was "in essence not meant for the guitar." Richards used no fuzz for the riff in the first several takes of the song (made in spring 1965). But, as he explained, "that riff needed to sustain itself."[26] A fuzz box provided the solution. Although Richards always considered the fuzz sound on "Satisfaction" a "bit of a gimmick," it generates much of the song's expressive power.[27] As David Dalton put it, the distorted riff "balances neatly on the borderline of menace, arrogance and incitement"— traits that entwine with the lyrics and Jagger's delivery.[28]

The music of "Satisfaction" oscillates between the two basic sonorities introduced in its opening. One is the grainy, medium-pitched buzzing and jangling blend of tambourine, snare drum, and fuzztone. The other is the smoother, darker sound of the bass. At the beginning of each verse, Richards switches off the fuzztone, and Jagger baby talks the line "I can't get no satisfaction," matching his vocal timbre to the bass and (now fuzz-less) guitar. Then he and Richards sing the words "'Cause I try and I try and I try and I try," singing higher and louder until their voices recede into the recorded mix of instrumental timbres. At the highest sung pitch the voices closely resemble the fuzztone, which Richards then switches back on. Jagger sings solo for the duration of the verse, matching his voice to the fuzztone timbre. He begins the next verse in baby talk and the entire process begins again. The polar sonorities of the rhythm section remain constant, with the melodic bass distinctly separated from the mechanistic snare drum and tambourine. But electric guitar and voice modulate from darker, throatier sonorities to brighter, raspier sonorities, then back again.

In the wake of "Satisfaction," fuzz became a standard color in the palette of electric guitar sounds by late 1965. "Distortion" controls and switches appeared on amplifiers, "fuzz" knobs on guitars. Several electronics companies began to issue their own versions of the fuzz effects pedals—with names ranging from the "Distortion Booster" and the "Tone Bender" to more metaphorical titles, such as the "Astrotone" and the "Pep Box." One could hear fuzz guitar in everything from cheaply made garage band records to slick pop and even prime-time television themes.[29]

By the end of 1966 the "distorted" sound of fuzz became a standard of stylistic purity—as suggested in the magazine *Popular Electronics*. For years the magazine showed amateurs how to build sound equipment that minimized distortion. Now an article suggested that fuzz was no longer a sign of damage but a hallmark of musical achievement: "As you listen to rock-'n'-roll by the big time performers, do you often wonder how they can get that fuzzy, raspy, piercing sound from an electric guitar while nonprofessional groups sound distinctively small-time?" The article went on to instruct amateurs how to build a device that would "sound as if [it] were tearing your speaker to shreds"—for less than three dollars.[30]

The Seattle-born guitarist Jimi Hendrix turned fuzz from a mannerism into an art. In late 1966 he moved to London, partly because he wanted to learn how to make his guitar sound like Beck's in "Heart Full of Soul."[31] Fortuitously, Hendrix met Roger Mayer after a January 1967 performance and experimented with some of Mayer's guitar effects-boxes in the dressing room. Thereafter, the two collaborated on fuzz and other effects until Hendrix's death in 1970. Mayer made over a dozen fuzz boxes for Hendrix, using several different designs customized to the sound Hendrix wanted. Hendrix became increasingly fastidious about fuzz; one of his road managers recalls him occasionally "screaming" that "this fuzz box isn't right" and trying several before he found the one with the right distortion.[32] As the flamboyant and virtuosic Hendrix became the most influential rock guitarist of the late 1960s, he alerted listeners to a widening palette of fuzz guitar subtleties.

Through fuzz the guitar assumed a new identity in rock music. What was the model for that identity? Robert Palmer suggests that amplified guitar sonorities such as fuzz turned the guitar into a huge bell—a resonant, overtone-laden chiming sound, full of a "clanging" that "ritually

invoke[s] sonic space."[33] And this is precisely what Link Wray had created in "Rumble"—a massive, carillon-like instrument that made the guitar sound both majestic and ominous. By simply defacing his amplifier
speaker, Wray seemed to intensify the natural overtones of metal strings,
creating what Carlos Santana called distortion's "rainbow effect."[34]

But there is ample historical evidence to suggest that distortion was
designed to change the guitar into a saxophone—not just a sustaining
instrument that can "solo" (a point that Palmer readily concedes), but a
wordless variant of the buzzing, roaring voice that exemplified African-
American ideals of singing as dramatic expression. While the saxophone
required a huge amount of physical exertion and dexterity to produce its
effects, the overdriven guitar made a similar sound with ease, as electrical energy supplanted bodily force. Players no longer had to coordinate
throat, tongue, and lungs. Instead they could turn on a switch and pick
the strings. One could play with the buzzing instrumental sound almost
endlessly (the only limitation being the durability of one's fingers).

This transformation assured rock's connection to what in the early
twentieth century was known as futurism—an aesthetic that glorifies the
sounds of technology. In the early twentieth century it was the technology of machinery; in the late, the technology of electronics. Thus, Johnny
Ramone explains that he "always wanted to get a sound like electricity"
on his guitar;[35] that fairly well sums up the futurist aesthetic. Moreover,
futurism seeks to incorporate some of the inadvertencies of technology
into its aesthetic—accidents, wear, breakage, ruin. Thus Andy Parypa
proudly notes that his distorted playing made his group the Sonics sound
"like a trainwreck"—a standard futurist image.[36]

Nevertheless, fuzz imbued the electric guitar with a soul it had not had.
As many guitarists have observed, distortion gave the guitar a sense of
personality—it "enlivened" the sound, gave it "character," to the point
where, as Eddie Kramer remarked, the particular distortion a player used
became "synonymous" with his or her "individuality."[37] In this way fuzz
arose from both the western tradition of developing a "singing" tone on
one's instruments and the African tradition of developing a distinctive
"personal" sound on one's instrument. From the mid-1960s on, electric
guitar players used countless variations on the fuzz idea to give themselves
unique, inimitable basic sonorities.

Through fuzz, a guitarist could give his or her instrument a voice. It
might be the transcendent, Middle-Eastern voice of "Heart Full of Soul,"
the brassy, urban voice of "Satisfaction," or anything in between. It might

even be the voice of another species—the barking of "Train Kept A-Roll-in'," the snarling of "Zip A Dee Doo Dah," or the buzzing of "2,000 Pound Bee." In every case, whatever the means of distortion, fuzz gave a guitar its own peculiar vocal "grain."

In the process, the guitar—once known as the "queen of instruments"—became an intensely masculine expressive tool. Through distortion its tone became, as one guitarist put it, "testosterone-laden."[38] That pretense of virility in the sound of the guitar corresponded to the aggressive images in the titles of guitar instrumentals—gangfights, rockets, trains, buzzsaws, and 2,000-pound bees.[39] The primary emotion was anger, a point observed even in Guitar Slim's overdriven playing, of which one observer commented, "it really sounds like he's mad at somebody."[40] The next generation found in fuzz the "overdriven-ness" of youth, the explosive hormonal diffusion in creatures whose social status was rigorously contained by their elders.

Through its aggressive, futuristic sound, fuzz was at the core of the machismo aesthetic of a new rock avant-garde—garage rock. Moreover, in psychedelic rock, the guitar would effectively exchange places with the voice, gaining its own multiple personalities through electronic special effects of which the fuzz box was only the beginning.

3 Avant Garage

"Garage" has become an indispensable adjective in the rock vocabulary. It appears regularly in record reviews, music histories and encyclopedias, and countless articles on obscure groups of the 1960s ("garage bands") and some of the music they played ("garage rock").[1] Some record stores have created "garage" sections. The titles of several recorded anthologies contain the term (*The Garage Zone, Garage Punk Unknowns, Girls in the Garage,* etc.) as do the liner notes to many others. Some students of popular music have even begun to use terms such as "neo-garage" and "post-garage."[2]

If "garage" is indispensable, it is also difficult to pin down. For example, what is a "garage band"? If the phrase denotes "a group who rehearsed in a garage," then most bands would qualify. If it means "a group who recorded in a garage"—that is, one of the many small urban or suburban studios built in converted garages—then most bands who made a demo record would qualify. The term becomes cloudier when one considers that writers apply it to bands of varying stature. Some sources apply the term "garage band" to relatively prominent groups, who by virtue of multiple charting records, strong album sales, national television exposure, or other factors, became known across the nation (Paul Revere and the Raiders, the Standells, the Seeds, the Five Americans, and the Kingsmen, to name a few). Other sources reserve the term for the so-called one-hit wonders, who may have had strong regional followings, but who, in national terms, "came up out of nowhere and scored one hit before going straight back there" (like Count Five or the Music Machine).[3] Still other sources apply the term to the various no-hit wonders who had regional followings, recorded a few songs, perhaps, but failed to "break" onto the national scene. Some writers discuss these latter groups with almost cultish admiration. Collectors pay high prices for the groups' records, which barely generated sales when they were new.

From a different perspective, Charlie Gillett writes that the term "garage band" should apply to two different types of groups, characterized by quite different styles.[4] The first type consists of groups primarily from the Pacific Northwest, the Midwest, and Texas. These groups began playing rhythm-and-blues-oriented rock several years before the British Invasion and continued playing it afterwards. The second type consists of the "national epidemic" of "groups formed by people who had only been inspired to learn an instrument after hearing the British records." These groups imitated the British Invasion groups, but typically knew little or nothing of the black artists who had inspired the British groups.

What Gillett does not mention is that his two types of groups were often the same groups in pre– and post–British Invasion incarnations. Consider the case of Paul Revere and the Raiders and their song "Louie, Go Home." When the Raiders wrote and recorded "Louie, Go Home" in 1964, the song was a sequel to their cover of Richard Berry's "Louie Louie." It had the typical New Orleans rhythm-and-blues sound of the 1950s: the instrumentation was piano, guitar, bass, drums, and, in the introduction, saxophone; the saxophone and bass doubled the left hand piano riff, the right hand of the piano played terse harmonic flourishes in the upper register; the tempo was moderate and the harmony consisted entirely of I, IV, and V chords.

Less than two years later, the Raiders re-recorded the song for their *Midnight Ride* album and revamped everything but the title. Now scored for guitar, bass, drums, small organ, and prominent tambourine, "Louie, Go Home" began with a two-line contrapuntal introduction that echoed the Stones' "Satisfaction." The chorus virtually transcribed the background vocals to the Yardbirds' "For Your Love" (harmony: I | ♭III | IV | ♭VI-♭VII). The tempo was much faster than the earlier version and the instrumental break featured a sitar-like fuzztone guitar, using changing modes (mixolydian moving to phrygian). In this remake the Raiders had essentially capitulated to the British invaders, just as did thousands of post–British Invasion garage bands that, as Burchill and Parsons put it, "erupted like coast-to-coast acne" in the mid-1960s.[5]

It was probably the Beatles' success that provoked thousands of young men, largely untrained in music, to suddenly come together as rock bands. As one band member explained it: "I was inspired by the Beatles like everyone else. I remember seeing them on the Ed Sullivan Show and thinking, 'Neat tunes. Simple. I can do that.'"[6] Another echoes the sentiment: "When the Beatles came along, we all stopped and looked at what we were doing and said, 'Hey—we could actually do this!'"[7] They came together as much to find companionship and recreation as to make art and money. As one observed about his first band, "We were probably like a million other high school bands in the world, doing our best, passing time, gettin' through school. Really, the group was just sort of something to do as a bunch of guys, our way of getting through."[8] And so they cleared some space in one member's garage, set up their drum sets, plugged in their small amplifiers, hooked-up their department-store electric guitars, and practiced songs.

The critical rite of passage for such a group was a "battle of the bands." A kind of event more or less born in the late 1950s, a battle of the bands brought together anywhere from two to two dozen local bands in a competition that could sometimes last all night. Each group would play a song or short set of songs and, after all had played, the audience would decide the winner by applauding loudest for their favorite. The grand prize for such an event usually included a recording session—which is how many a garage band happened to make a record at all.[9] The records could then promote the band's live performances (and vice versa). But despite the competition for what Robert Dalley calls "territorial bragging rights," these groups were ultimately concerned more with building a fellowship than vanquishing their rivals. As one recalls, "We were all trying to do our best [but] I don't know of any one-upmanship as you might think. It was more like camaraderie than competition, 'cause we were all in the same boat trying to make it in music."[10]

But along with the camaraderie came an attitude for which "garage" provided an apt metaphor. A garage is a rougher, dirtier place than where humans typically reside; a place to store heavy machinery and marginally useful possessions. It is a place of noise and alienation, a psychological space as much as a physical one. In this light "garage band" implies a distancing from more respectable bands (and from more respectable social enterprises in general). The Clash put it well in the chorus to one of their early songs: "We are a garage band / We come from garage land." Yet garage bands may have also seen themselves as a new musical elite—authentic practitioners of music on the cutting edge of an emerging culture.

In retrospect, garage bands seem the avant garde of sixties rock—"avant garde" in the sense of a self-conscious community whose participants insist on their independence from the masses and the rightfulness of their artistic path. Groups like the Rolling Stones and the Yardbirds—British icons of many American garage bands—saw themselves not just as entertainers, says Giorgio Gomelsky, onetime manager of both groups, but as part of an authentic art movement, even a "chosen people": "Like the existentialists in Paris or the beat generation, Kerouac's people. Every minority springs out of a desire to go back to a form of authenticity and hence it creates a logarithmic process, it multiplies itself. Four people the first night, eight the second. When you sense that, you know you're on to a sensibility, a wavelength that you cannot go wrong on."[11]

Two things that distinguish an avant garde, according to Renato Poggioli, scholar of such movements, are activism and antagonism. Poggioli explains: "often [an avant garde] takes shape and agitates for no other end than its own self, out of the sheer joy of dynamism, a taste for action, a sportive enthusiasm, and the emotional fascination of adventure."[12] Among garage bands—no less than among the futurists (Poggioli's model)—the aesthetics of *activism* manifests itself in two somewhat distinct forms. First, it worships speed, particularly the speed of mechanization and technology. Second, it worships virility and brutish masculinity. As the futurist Marinetti wrote, "we [futurists] want to exalt aggressive action . . . the smack and the punch"; he urged his fellow artists, "Let us be barbarians! . . . Hail the savagery . . . and the fury of muscular, exalting and fortifying dance . . . in the name of health, force, will power and virility."[13] How garage rock manifests such sentiments will become clear.

Avant-garde movements also direct *antagonism* toward conservative values and even toward their own audience. According to Poggioli, this antagonism is individualistic—the "revolt of the 'unique' *against* society"—and at the same time communal, the "solidarity within the community of rebels and libertarians."[14] Avant garde antagonism flouts conventions, especially the most visible conventions of dress and grooming.[15] It also shows contempt for the standard paths of success and career-building.

The Rolling Stones embodied the antagonism to which garage bands aspired. The Stones and their manager (after Gomelsky), Andrew Loog Oldham, cultivated this attitude on the theory that "for every star there is an anti-star."[16] If the Beatles could succeed by being cute, witty, nicely dressed, and musically smooth, then others could succeed by being the opposite—homely, uncouth, sloppy, and musically rough. They defined their antagonism, and indeed the musical rhetoric of garage antagonism, in songs like "Stupid Girl" (1966), "Under My Thumb" (1966), and especially their hit "(I Can't Get No) Satisfaction." Basing the song's refrain on Muddy Waters's "I Can't Be Satisfied," Jagger and co-writer Keith Richards adapted a rural black assertion of personal dissatisfaction into an urban white assertion of cultural repulsion. In text and sonority, the song codified the Stones' flouting of middle-class values.

American garage bands absorbed the Stones' brand of antagonism, and often directed it at the implied listener—usually a woman, but sometimes anyone or everyone. Some song titles rebuke and despise—"I Can't Stand This Love, Goodbye," "Baby Get Lost," "Leave Me Alone," "Go On, Leave," and "You'll Never Be My Girl"; they complain of being trammeled—"I'm Not Your Stepping Stone," "Don't Tread On Me," "Don't Crowd Me," "[You're] Pushin' Too Hard"; and they often menace—"Nothing'll Stand in My Way," "Be Forewarned." While pop groups oozed with the bliss of love, garage bands bristled with the energy of contempt.

Both activism and antagonism, hallmarks of avant garde movements, permeated garage rock and the mentality of those who played it—on the semantic and sociological levels at least. But it was the music that bound the participants together in a cohesive, symbol-laden community, one that would revolutionize the culture of both hemispheres. We have discussed the singing and fuzzy guitars that characterize much of garage rock. Here we will focus on the beat, the chords, and the riffs that intertwined in garage rock, forming a web of activist/antagonist codes.

*

In much western music the listener does not hear the beat overtly, but perceives it as a chronometric implication beneath the surface of the actual rhythms.[17] But rock 'n' roll drummers and rhythm guitarists (as had their rhythm and blues predecessors) blatantly stated the beat—leading some critics to condemn the music for its vulgar overstating of the obvious. But the pounding beat of rock 'n' roll functioned structurally as the bedrock of a multi-layered entity. The beat provided a plain surface against which the quirkily shaped melodic lines of rock 'n' roll came into relief. The melodic rhythms usually abounded in uneven divisions of the pulse, small accelerations and decelerations, and irregular accents. These free lines made counterpoint against their rigid opposite, the primitive utterance known as the beat. The two needed each other to make an aesthetic whole.

Three kinds of beat shaped rock 'n' roll. The most common is the "backbeat." Bill Haley summarizes it: "drop the first and third beats and accentuate the second and fourth."[18] The backbeat derived from various African-American styles, especially rhythm and blues and swing-style jazz. Its charm was in creating a responsorial effect with the "true" (i.e., metric) accents.[19]

The second kind of beat that shaped rock 'n' roll comes from country music and gospel. A close relation to the backbeat, the "offbeat" (or "two-step") accentuates the second half of every beat. Both offbeat and backbeat emphasize the "wrong" part of the rhythm—in one case the "wrong" part of a beat (1 *and* 2 *and* . . .), in the other case the "wrong" part of a meter (1 *2* 3 *4*). The tempo of a song could sometimes make it difficult to tell whether accents were offbeats or backbeats. As rhythmic theorists Cooper and Meyer observe, listeners normally interpret a musical beat as having a moderate tempo.[20] The resting human pulse defines a "moderate tempo"; in music, fast beats suggest an active human pulse, but extremely fast beats actually tend to divide up and be heard in pairs because as individual beats they exceed what the human heart can feasibly maintain.[21] Thus, in the case of some gospel and country music one cannot always discern whether the primary stresses of the rhythm section are offbeats of a moderately slow pulse or backbeats of a pulse twice that fast.

The offbeat moved from gospel music into "soul" music via performers such as Ray Charles ("Talkin' About You," 1956; "Leave My Woman Alone," 1958) and Sam Cooke ("Happy in Love," 1957), and groups such as the Isley Brothers ("Shout," 1959) and Little Anthony and the Imperials ("I'm Alright," 1959)—all of whom secularized black church music by giving new lyrics to gospel tunes. Rock 'n' roll recordings feature the offbeat as well, especially some of Chuck Berry's country-influenced records such as "You Can't Catch Me" (1955), "Maybellene" (1955), "Too Much Monkey Business" (1956), "Oh Baby Doll" (1957), and "Beautiful Delilah" (1958). Early films of Bo Diddley illustrate the ambiguity of backbeats vs. offbeats in rock 'n' roll: they show him moving his body to a leisurely tempo against the apparent drum backbeats that move twice as fast. Do the accents fall on the weak beats of fast measures (as the drum playing suggests) or on the second half of each beat (as his body language suggests)?[22]

In many cases performers changed from backbeats to offbeats at the end of a song—a practice best described as "pseudo-double time."[23] Gospel music abounded with this practice: players often followed the final chorus with a long coda that doubled the speed of the backbeats, effectively turning them to offbeats, while keeping the harmonic rhythm the same.[24] Jazz and soul followed suit—consider Ray Charles's rendition of "I Got a Woman" at the Newport Jazz Festival, 1958. In the 1960s, rock 'n' roll and pop artists sometimes used pseudo-double time for codas (as in the ending of the Crystals' "He's a Rebel," 1962). Occasionally, a shift from backbeats to offbeats signaled the arrival of something other than the coda (Paul Anka's "Diana," 1957, uses offbeats only in the *bridge* of the song).

A third kind of rock 'n' roll beat is what Dave Laing calls the "rhythmic monad": the players accent every beat. According to Laing, this equal accentuation—strong-strong-strong-strong—creates "a state of entropy (or perfection)," depending on one's point of view.[25] By its stubborn persistence it connotes pure power. Some theorists have tried to characterize various patterns of accent; Deryck Cooke, for example, suggests that triple meter connotes "relaxation and abandonment" and duple meter connotes "control or rigidity."[26] But the rhythmic monad seems almost expressionless: each beat seems isolated, individual, existing only for itself. Yet each beat is completely integrated into a larger, implicitly infinite, group of equivalent beats.

One can trace the monad from urban blues to Memphis soul and Motown. Several of the mid-1950s Chess recordings of Muddy Waters ("Long Distance Call," "Honey Bee," "She Moves Me," "Still a Fool," and "Standing Around Crying," to name a few) project an undifferentiated series of accents—loud, slow, constant thumps. In the mid-1960s, this uniform beat found its way into fast dance-oriented musics. Known as a "stomp" beat, it appears in several Stax-Volt singles, the earliest of which is William Bell's "Just As I Thought" (1963).[27] An emphatic snare on every beat—and no compensating backbeat—subsequently appears in Floyd Newman's "Frog Stomp" (1963) and the Mad Lads' "Sidewalk Surf" (1964). Motown recordings of the mid-1960s further popularized the monad.[28] The Supremes' "Come See About Me" (1964) uses miked handclaps to accent every beat; in the following year snare attacks on every beat appear in Martha Reeves and the Vandellas' "Nowhere to Run," the Supremes' "Stop! In the Name of Love," the Four Tops' "The Same Old Song," and Stevie Wonder's "Uptight." By 1966 the equalization of accent by snare attack on every beat had become a standard feature of Motown recordings. It was probably designed to project the beat clearly on even the smallest, most inexpensive speakers—that is, those in automobiles. The result irresistibly demanded attention (if not always respect).

The British rhythm and blues-based groups that inspired American garage bands in the 1960s used three principal beat techniques: the rhythmic monad, pseudo-double time, and a derivative of it, the rave-up. As one of the first white groups to cover Stax-Volt and Motown recordings, the Rolling Stones brought the rhythmic monad to an even larger audience than it had before. In the spring of 1965 they recorded "Satisfaction," which gained much of its drive from the snare accentuation of every beat. In 1966 they continued using the rhythmic monad in "Paint It, Black" (verse only) and "Stupid Girl."

But British groups concentrated less on the accentuation of the beat than on the speed of the beat. Although rarely discussed in scholarly analyses, tempo clearly determines a great deal of the expressive nature of a song. As Cooke puts it, "The effect of tempo on emotional expression is clearly all-important."[29] Chicago bluesmen such as Muddy Waters played at ponderous tempi to display a sense of strength; the slower tempi represented more brute mass than faster ones could. Thus Waters slows down the tempo of Bo Diddley's "I'm a Man" (♩ = 80–85) for his quasi-cover entitled "Mannish Boy" (♩ = 70–75). As Dave Marsh aptly explains, "Muddy picks up Bo's basic beat, but he slows the tempo, seemingly holding it down with main strength"; and while Diddley's declaration of being a "full-grown man" was "a fairly innocuous novelty," Waters's was "leering and imposing."[30] But when the Yardbirds covered the song they almost doubled Diddley's original tempo (♩ = 140–145).[31] This transformed one kind of manliness into another. Diddley and Waters conceive of virility as a slow, resonant pounding; the Yardbirds reconceive it as an energetic, mechanistic beat. One emphasizes force, the other action.[32]

The sort of acceleration used by the Yardbirds for "I'm a Man" typifies many British groups of the period, who seemed peculiarly obsessed with speed as an expression of youthful energy. Despite their producers' request not to do so, the Stones rendered blues and rock standards hastily, as if sheer zeal could make up for what they lacked in stylistic purity.[33] In their 1964 cover of Chuck Berry's "Carol," for example, they accelerate the pulse from ♩ = 158 to ♩ = 175 (they also add offbeat accentuation); in their cover of Buddy Holly and the Crickets' "Not Fade Away," they accelerate from ♩ = 90–95 to ♩ = 115; in their cover of Waters's "I Just Wanna Make Love to You" they more than double the original tempo. In their own songs, the Stones often played at tempi that made it difficult to tell if offbeats or backbeats were being used (see, for example, "Little by Little," 1964).

Still, it was the Yardbirds who, more than perhaps any of their peers, demonstrated a quasi-futuristic love of sheer speed. As an energetic club band, they signed their first record contract in 1964. But they were stymied by an inability to reproduce the raw energy in the studio: "You'd do a blockbuster at the Crawdaddy," said one band member, "and then you'd come out of the studio with this very clean sound. It just didn't relate; it was very schizophrenic."[34] So they took the unusual step of making their first album a live album. This album, *Five Live Yardbirds,* displays their characteristically frenetic tempi and their patented "rave-up" technique.

The rave-up was a pseudo-double time section with a corresponding intensification of dynamics (the drummer attacked the ride cymbal ferociously on each eighth-note, rising in crescendo until the music reached a dynamic climax). Typically, if the rave-up occurred at the sole instrumental break in the song, the music would die down and prepare for the reentry of the lead voice; if it came at the end of a song, the music stopped abruptly at the dynamic climax. Wherever it occurred, the rave-up made a small narrative curve that introduced a basic conflict (backbeats vs. offbeats), drove that conflict to a climax (by getting more and more raucous), then resolved it (by returning it to a "normal" beat). Through this technique the Yardbirds created a rock mannerism; sometimes the rave-up seemed the whole point of the song.

The Stones and the Yardbirds saturated their music with rhythmic intensity. American garage bands imitated them, favoring rapid, overheated tempi, offbeats, and rave-ups. Two examples from Paul Revere and the Raiders show how they could use such rhythmic intensifications to enhance the expression of the text. In "Steppin' Out" the Raiders use pseudo-double time to augment the threatening tone of the bridge—"I told you once, I told you twice / Don't you come around or else I'll put you on ice." In "I'm Not Your Stepping Stone" they use a rave-up to support Mark Lindsay's roaring repetitions of the single phrase "not your stepping stone!"[35]

Finally, garage bands embraced the rhythmic monad, not just to imitate the Stones and their precursors, but also to make drumming easy: even drummers who could not roll or improvise fills could produce an "authentic" monad sound. While crude, the constant accentuation allowed drummers to express the activism and antagonism that inspired the movement.[36]

*

Most observers relegate harmony in garage rock to a matter of musical ineptitude—groups merely played the few chords they knew. Understandably, such observers spend almost no time dealing with the harmony of the style. Dave Laing, for example, entitles his book on punk (the 1970s sequel to garage rock) *One Chord Wonders;*[37] correspondingly, he never discusses harmony in the text. An aspiring garage rock musician, writes Nigel Strange, needed only to "learn a couple of chords on guitar."[38] And Peter Blecha assesses the recordings of a well-known garage band in this way: "Three chords, two tracks, and one hell of a band."[39]

Such statements can be misleading. First, they overstate the limitations of the groups' harmonic vocabulary. Second, they imply that the small vocabulary has to do with ignorance or lack of ambition, when in fact most garage rockers could (and did) learn many chords. But their decision to restrict the harmonic vocabulary must be seen in most cases as a matter of choice—as Laing suggests about punk rockers, "the 'incompetence' of [these] musicians was more rhetorical than actual."[40] The harmony of garage rock actually supports the garage bands' activist/antagonist point of view. Yet earlier styles foreshadowed garage rock harmony: blues and rock 'n' roll artists also played primarily one-, two-, and three-chord songs.

Harmony is indeed negligible in the simpler blues forms, which derived from the "field hollers" of the rural south. Songs like "Baby, Please Don't Go" contain only one "chord"; the interest of the song lies more in the unequal phrase lengths of the text, the nuances of the melody, and the energy of the responsories. Various urban blues recordings in the early 1950s (e.g., by Muddy Waters and John Lee Hooker) do the same. Other blues songs contain a simple two-measure melodic riff—a short, recurring melodic idea—that implies only a single harmony. That line typically intertwines with the singer's contrapuntal improvisations (see Howlin' Wolf's "Smokestack Lightning"). Bo Diddley's influential eponymous song—itself probably a transcription of a much older song—is also of the harmonically severe one-chord sort, except that, between verses, the harmony oscillates between I and its lower neighbor a whole step below, $\flat$VII. All such harmonic practice suggests the ultimate in self-constraint, a doggedness, a persistence, even a macho ability to "sustain."

Some three-chord progressions involved the chords I, $\flat$III, and IV. Although there are precedents in blues recordings, the records that really established such progressions in the ears of a mass audience were the Everly Brothers' first two hits "Bye Bye Love" and "Wake Up Little Susie" (both 1957). In the first record, the Everlys play the one-measure progression [I-$\flat$III-IV] as an introduction to the whole song. In the second record, they play the two-measure progression [I | $\flat$III-IV-$\flat$III] as an introduction to each verse.

The more common three-chord progressions, however, involve the primary triads (I, IV, and V). The twelve-bar blues progression is the classic example. While it contains only those three chords, it deploys them in a remarkable way:

MM.	1–4	5–6	7–8	9	10	11–12
	I	IV	I	V	IV	[I]

As one can see, the progression accelerates in its harmonic rhythm through the first ten measures. The final two measures often contain a "turnaround" progression, with harmonic changes on every beat in the eleventh (e.g., [I-V7/IV-IV-iv]) then I and V for two beats each in the twelfth. Behaving like a lopsided wheel, the twelve-bar blues gains harmonic momentum toward the end of the cycle then loses it as the cycle begins again. Moreover, the motion of the dominant to the subdominant in measures 9–10 (often omitted in rhythm and blues) thwarts the expected forward motion. The dominant yields to the subdominant, "weakening" the progression (according to classical theory).

The twelve-bar blues sometimes provided a map for transpositions of the [I-♭III-IV] progression. In Booker T. and the MGs' "Green Onions" (1962), for example, a bass figure suggesting the latter progression is mapped onto each harmony of the blues progression.[41] When organist Booker T. Jones uses major chords to harmonize that bass line, he ends up with this set of chords: I, ♭III, IV, V, ♭VI, ♭VII. This set consists of major chords on each degree of the minor pentatonic scale, plus one (♭VI).

How did garage rock harmony relate to its blues and rock 'n' roll percursors? To begin with, garage bands created relatively few one-chord songs. But they often relied on simple oscillations between two chords. (These oscillations seldom proceed through an entire song but rather through one section of the form, usually the verse). For such oscillations they preferred I-♭VII or I-IV.

The progression I-♭VII was not uncommon in folk music, but had rarely appeared in rock 'n' roll, the most notable exceptions being "Bo Diddley" and the Champs' instrumental hit "Tequila" (1958).[42] In the countless garage rock records that use it, however, the oscillation of I and ♭VII gives the illusion of motion, but always the ambivalent motion of a musical "neighbor"—step away, step back, step away, step back, and so on. This kind of musical running-in-place suited the activism of the style. It could also support a text: the Seeds' "Pushin' Too Hard" (perhaps the best-known example of a song whose harmony consists *only* of I-♭VII oscillation), suggests an equilibrium, a harmonic paralysis that illustrates the frustration expressed in the lyrics "All I want is to just be free".[43]

The I-IV oscillation derives from such oscillations found in countless Memphis soul recordings (usually in verses). Whereas the I-♭VII oscillation merely embellishes the tonic harmony, the I-IV oscillation suggests the back-and-forth motion of a simple machine. While displaying some superficial motion, this oscillation achieves no goal or resolution. It appears to be mere harmonic "action"—an expression of restlessness for its own sake.

Many garage songs use three-chord ostinatos in which ♭III serves as a stepping stone to the subdominant, with planed harmonies à la the Everly Brothers. Ascending two-measure patterns featuring I, ♭III, and IV appear frequently, expanding the idea of oscillation into a large "wave motion" of harmony—two chords move to a third chord, then back away from it: I-♭III | IV-♭III, for example (as found in the Sonics' "Boss Hoss," the Emperors' "I Want My Woman," and the Traits' "High on a Cloud," where it appears in 6/8). Variants of this progression abound. There are expanded versions (the Brothers Grimm's "You'll Never Be Mine": I-♭III | IV | IV-♭III | I; the Standells' "Try It": I | ♭III-IV-♭III | IV-I | I) or contracted versions (the Floating Bridge's "It Don't Mean a Thing to Me": I-♭III-IV-♭III as a one-measure recurring idea). Some prolong the tonic at the beginning (the Hangmen's "What a Girl Can't Do": I | ♭III-IV-♭III, borrowed from the Animals' oft-covered "I'm Crying?"), or at end (Byron and the Mortals' "Do You Believe Me?": I-♭III-IV-♭III | I). Still others prolong the subdominant, with the return of ♭III necessarily omitted (the Chocolate Watchband's "Are You Gonna Be There?": I-♭III | IV-iv, taken from the Yardbirds' influential "For Your Love").[44]

Other two-measure ostinatos contain the *primary* triads, blending the "wave motion" idea with the harmonic content of the twelve-bar blues. "Louie Louie" (I-IV | V-IV) is the classic example, one explicitly echoed in the Wailers' "You Weren't Using Your Head," the McCoys' "Hang On Sloopy," and countless others.[45]

In most of the progressions we have discussed, the subdominant gains great harmonic weight. In other progressions, the subtonic enhances that weight. Consider one of the most-played songs in the garage repertoire, Them's "Gloria." Its one-measure harmonic ostinato, [I-♭VII-IV], maps the characteristic falling-second/falling-fourth progression of the blues (V-IV-I) onto the subdominant (I-♭VII-IV).[46] Thus, when the progression returns to the tonic, one hears "double plagal" motion. The subtonic loses its more common role as a lower neighbor to the tonic and becomes a subdominant to the subdominant, proceeds to the real subdominant, then to the tonic: [I-IV/IV-IV].[47]

In "Empty Heart" the Rolling Stones treat ♭VII as IV/IV but follow the IV chord with a V, then drive strongly to the tonic: [I-♭VII | IV-V]. Although the progression may have appeared in earlier songs, it apparently entered the harmonic vocabulary of rock through the Stones, who attached it to the beginning of their cover of the Valentinos' "It's All Over Now" (1964). Barry Mann and Cynthia Weill later used the progression at the end of each verse of their song "We Gotta Get Out of This Place," a hit for the Animals in 1966. Mann and Weill subsequently wrote "Hungry" for Paul Revere and the Raiders, which repeats the "Empty Heart" progression throughout the chorus. The Wilde Knights picked up the progression for their song "Just Like Me" (1965), playing it in all but the bridge of that song. When the Raiders covered it, they cut the bridge, leaving the song entirely in the ostinato form of "Empty Heart."

After ♭VII became IV/IV, it seemed only natural that ♭III should sometimes function, in effect, as the subdominant of the subdominant of the subdominant—that is, ♭III = IV/♭VII, with the ♭VII functioning in turn as IV/IV. Consider "Fluctuation" by the Shades of Night (not to be confused with the Shadows of Knight), which logically extends the "Gloria" progression into [I-♭III | ♭VII-IV]. The result is clearly heard as *triple* plagal motion: they approach the tonic at the beginning of each two-measure segment by no less than three falling fourths. Finally, a few groups tried *quadruple* plagal motion (♭VI-♭III-♭VII-IV-I), a progression popularized by one of garage rock's best-loved songs, "Hey Joe"—about which we will have much more to say in the next chapter.

Chord progressions in which the chord roots form chains of perfect fourths grow out of a musical culture based on the guitar, an instrument tuned in fourths (except for one string). Previously, the guitar existed in a western musical culture more or less based on the keyboard for its harmonic thinking. But in rock the guitar dominated and so its natural properties led to new harmonic norms. Chains of fourth-related chord roots come in part from the very act of tuning the instruments: as players tuned up their guitars, they inevitably became accustomed to the sound of these chains.

*

Riffs give the listener a simple but memorable musical idea to retain well after the song ends. While riffs are often melodic ideas, garage bands preferred overtly percussive *rhythmic* riffs, since they required far less dexterity: a guitarist need only finger a chord with the left hand, then execute

the rhythmic riff with the right.[48] Two archetypal rhythmic riffs dominated the genre, both of them with common characteristics: the "Bo Diddley" rhythm and the "Louie Louie" rhythm.

The "Bo Diddley" riff (Ex. 1) derived from the West African "patted
juba" or "hambone" rhythm, popularized among black American street
workers via the phrase "shave-and-a-haircut, six bits." Although the riff
appeared in earlier recordings (e.g., the Andrews Sisters' "Rum and Coca
Cola," 1944), Bo Diddley brought it to the attention of rock 'n' roll players through his eponymous recording of 1958.[49] Buddy Holly took it for
his "Not Fade Away" (1957), as did Them in "Mystic Eyes" (1965). In most
cases the "Bo Diddley" rhythmic riff supports a single harmony.

Example 1. The "Bo Diddley" Rhythmic Riff

The riff appears in many garage recordings, including the hit single "I
Want Candy" by the Strangeloves (1965). By the mid-1960s some garage
bands began to use this riff to delineate the verse ("Ain't It the Truth" by
the Bootmen; "Guaranteed Love" by Limey and the Yanks) or the chorus
("Take a Look at Me" by Mr. Lucky and the Gamblers) from the rest of the
song.[50] In such instances, the single harmony of earlier incarnations gives
way to a short, common garage harmonic progression. In "Bad Woman,"
for example, the Fallen Angels combine this riff with the wave-motion
ostinato [I-IV | ♭VII-IV].

At least as common as the "Bo Diddley" riff was the "Louie Louie"
rhythmic riff (Ex. 2), which Richard Berry, the author of "Louie Louie,"
took from Rene Touzet's "El Loco Cha Cha" (1956).[51] After "Louie Louie"
caught on with Northwest rock 'n' roll bands in the early 1960s, dozens
of groups recorded it, including the Kingsmen (whose version became
their biggest hit in 1963). While "Louie Louie," as we have seen, used the
wave-motion harmonic progression [I-IV | V-IV], new songs appeared that
superimposed the rhythmic riff onto other common garage progressions.
In the chorus and instrumental break of "Just Like Me," for instance, Paul
Revere and the Raiders combine the "Louie Louie" rhythmic riff with the
"Empty Heart" harmonic progression. Still other groups kept the *harmony* of "Louie Louie," but slightly modified the rhythm. The Troggs, often
considered Britain's first garage band, use such a modified "Louie Louie"
riff in their hit "Wild Thing" (1966).

Example 2. The "Louie Louie" Rhythmic Riff

Perhaps the most durable rhythmic riff among garage bands was a simple rhythmic figure taken from pop vocal recordings of the early 1960s. It consisted of dotted-quarter/eighth notes in alternation at a tempo of about ♩=70; these notes either persisted unbroken or, more typically, lasted for six beats, then changed to even quarter notes for the final two beats. Popularized in such recordings as the Four Seasons' "Sherry" (1962) and the Righteous Brothers' "You've Lost That Lovin' Feeling" (1964), this latter rhythmic riff dominates the song "My Girl Sloopy." A staple of garage bands, "Sloopy" was first recorded by the Vibrations, then covered by many other groups, including the Yardbirds and the New Colony Six. But it is best known as a hit by the McCoys, retitled "Hang On Sloopy" (1965).

The same rhythmic ostinato—with or without its seminal two-measure harmonic accompaniment (I-IV | V-IV) appears in various other garage recordings, often with power chords in the guitar instead of the single notes found in some earlier recordings. And consider how bands superimposed standard garage progressions onto the "Sloopy" riff:

The Rumors ("Hold Me Now"): [I-IV | ♭VII-IV]

The Emperors ("I Want My Woman"): [I-♭III | IV-♭III]

Kit and the Outlaws ("Don't Tread On Me"): [I-♭III | V-IV-♭III]

The Weeds ("It's Your Time"): [I-♭III | IV-I]

Meanwhile, the Remains, in "Hard Time Comin'," play the "Sloopy" riff as the undergirding for a simple I-♭VII oscillation that gives way to a rave-up.

Garage bands created garage rock by combining fuzz and post-Jagger vocalisms with the harmonic and rhythmic elements we have examined. Consider, for example, one of the most popular garage rock songs, "Psychotic Reaction" by Count Five (1966). It begins with a fuzztone riff apparently taken from the introduction to Johnny Rivers's version of Mose Allison's "Seventh Son" (1965).[52] Accompanying the fuzztone, the drummer plays a rhythmic monad on the bass drum. The rhythm guitarist begins a I-♭VII oscillation and lead singer Kenn Ellner sings with Jaggeresque disembodiment and dialect. After the words "and it [the psychotic reaction] feels like this" the group plays a rave-up taken directly from the Yard-birds' "I'm a Man."[53] After the rave-up, they play as before, Ellner refers even more explicitly to the Stones (singing the line "I can't get satisfaction"), and the rave-up returns to close the song. Moreover, the entire song is drenched in "phasing," a technique that links it to psychedelic style (about which more later).

What would such a song as "Psychotic Reaction"—or the thousands like it in the garage repertoire—have to do with the idea of an avant garde? Its musical traits express activism and antagonism yet serve to build a community. The rhythmic monad exemplifies a pure, quasi-futurist pattern of mechanistic attacks. The tempo and the harmony both suggest activism: the acceleration of the beat connotes velocity for its own sake; the oscillating harmony connotes restless energy without direction. Yet "Psychotic Reaction," like similar songs of the style, strives to create a family of resemblances. Garage bands, after all, built a musical community by wearing their various genetic codes on their sleeves. In garage rock, riffs, fuzz, and other musical details serve as musical signs, conversational details passed from recording to recording in a way that tied the whole garage movement together.

Keith Richards set forth the underlying rationale for those groups who banded together despite limited technique: "Music is one of those things you can never get to the bottom of. . . . No matter how limited you are, you can still find variations and things that please you."[54] Garage bands discovered the potentially endless variety in their minimal technique. And ironically, their dogged devotion to the fundamentals fostered the more "sophisticated" rock that would follow. For by exploring the variations within the simplest of materials garage bands helped other rock musicians realize how rich was the musical quarry they were digging.

4 The Not-So-Average "Joe"

There are good reasons to study the song "Hey Joe." As Lester Bangs said, for a few years in the 1960s "everybody and his . . . brother not only recorded but claimed to have written" "Hey Joe."[1] Between 1966 and 1969 countless rock bands included the song in their repertoire because of its catchy, continuous chord progression, not to mention the machismo of its text. Hundreds of artists recorded it and at least five different recordings became regional, national, or international hits. Dave Marsh suggests another reason to study "Hey Joe": the song "probably fit[s] the academic definition of the 'folk process' better than any other rock and roll song."[2] Almost no one seemed sure of who wrote the song and many people claimed that they, in fact, had. Anyone who wants to see how a song can come to belong to everyone—and no one—as it travels from artist to artist should consider "Hey Joe." Finally, the song is a stylistic prism: the transformations it underwent reveal the full spectrum of rock enthusiasms during the late 1960s. It not only traversed folk rock, garage rock, soul, psychedelic, and mainstream pop during those years, it continued to adapt to the styles of the 1970s through the 1990s. Its position in the repertoire, its unusual history, and its constantly changing details all make "Hey Joe" worthy of close attention.

*

To begin to understand the "folk process" in "Hey Joe," consider briefly four phenomena in American music: question and answer songs, crime ballads, "hey" songs in general, and "Hey Joe" songs in particular. Dozens of Anglo-American folksong texts consist of a series of questions and answers. Some use simple third-person narratives—he asked this, someone answered, and so on—as in "Billy Barlow":

> What shall I hunt says Dan'l to Joe . . .
> Hunt for a rat, says Billy Barlow
>
> How shall I get him, says Dan'l to Joe
> Go borrow a gun, says Billy Barlow.[3]

But in other cases, the singer assumes the identity of both speakers in the dialogue—the first asking the questions, the second answering them—as in "Billy Boy": "Where have you been, Billy Boy, Billy Boy? / . . . / I've been down the lane to see Miss Betsy Jane."[4] Some popular songs in the twentieth century—such as the World War I song "Hinky Dinky, Parlay-Voo?"—follow the same pattern: "Oh, landlord, have you got a daughter, parlay voo? / . . . / Oh, yes, I have a daughter fair."[5]

Like question and answer songs, crime ballads abound in Anglo-American folk music. Some of these ballads—usually about murderers—address the criminal directly. For example, in many songs about the legendary "Stagger Lee" (a.k.a. "Stagolee" or "Stack'o'Lee") the singer sings not *about* but *to* the vengeful Lee, who killed Billy Lyon with a "blue steel forty-four."[6] A few crime ballads even use the question-answer format, as in "Edward." In the first line Edward's father asks: "What makes that blood on the point of your knife? My son now tell to me." Edward responds: "It is the blood of my old gray mare who plowed the fields for me." The song reveals (through a series of questions and answers) that it is really the blood of Edward's brother John. When the truth is discovered at the song's end, Edward flees on a boat to "sail the ocean round."[7]

Although the word "hey" appears in many songs as a nonsense syllable—"hey diddle diddle," "hey nonny nonny," etc.—it usually functions as a call to some imaginary character. Consider the dozens of "hey" songs that appeared on the popular charts in the 1950s and 1960s. Usually a male narrator addresses a female with "hey": three versions of the song "Hey Girl" have made the Top 40, as have three different songs named "Hey[!] Baby," and four different songs named "Hey[!] Little Girl." Sometimes the "hey" addresses a male ("Hey Jude"), although typically a male in a distinct vocation ("Hey Mr. Banjo," "Hey Harmonica Man," "Hey, Western Union Man," "[Hey] Mr. Tambourine Man," etc.). More than any other male, the object of the "hey" is an imaginary character named Joe.

To post–World War II Americans the name "Joe" seemed to represent everyman. They colloquially referred to a typical male as an "average Joe"; a decent fellow was "a good Joe"; a good soldier was "G.I. Joe." (The name was even applied to common food products: a cup of coffee was "a cup of Joe"; a variant on the hamburger was a "sloppy Joe.") In the early 1950s, television star Jackie Gleason helped popularize the mythical Joe in his "Joe the Bartender" sketches. In these sketches, as in their vaudevillian precursors, bar patrons initiated conversations with the bartender by the salutation "Hey Joe!"

Not surprisingly, given the almost archetypal status of the name, American songwriters composed dozens of "Hey Joe" songs. During the years 1947–57, more than a song a year with "Hey Joe" in the title was registered for copyright; thereafter the number of registered "Hey Joe" titles increased dramatically.[8] Some of these were dances, including the "Hey Joe Calypso" (1957) and the "Hey Joe Polka" (1961). Some contained calls for the imaginary Joe to get busy: "Hey! Joe! The Water's Boilin'" (1947), "Hey Up, Joe! On Your Way," "Hey Joe, Close That Door" (both 1953). Others asked questions of Joe: "Hey Joe, Wadda You Know" (1948, and later variants), "Hey, Joe! Why Donna You Work So Hot?" (1959), "Hey! Joe! Why You Steal the Banana?" (1962).

In 1953 country singer Carl Smith had a hit record entitled "Hey Joe!" It begins: "Hey Joe! Where'd you find that pearly girly? / Where'd you get that jolly dolly? / How'd you rate that dish I wish was mine?" The singer goes on to warn Joe that although he "ain't no heel," he's going to try to steal the girl away from Joe. This record sold over a million copies for Smith, prompting other country singers to cover the song. Even pop singer Frankie Laine included it in his nightclub act, where it became one of his "most requested songs."[9]

In January 1962, William Moses Roberts Jr. copyrighted yet another song entitled "Hey Joe." This song, however, rejected the lightheartedness of earlier "Hey Joe" songs. A crime ballad with a question-answer format, Roberts's song dwelt on jealousy and retribution. It depicted a series of encounters between the singer and Joe; each verse consisted of a single couplet:

Hey Joe, where you goin' with that money in your hand?
Chasin' my woman, she run off with another man.

Going downtown, buy me a forty-four.
When I get through that woman won't run no more.

Hey Joe, what are you gonna do?
Take my pistol, and kill her before I'm through.

Hey Joe, I heard you shot your woman dead.
Yes, I did; got both of them lying in that bed
   (or: smack through the head)

Hey Joe, where do you think you'll go?
Leaving here, think I'll go to Mexico.

Yes I'm going, going where I can be free.
'Cause ain't no hangman gonna put no noose on me.[10]

The harmonic accompaniment to these words consists of the same four-measure major-chord progression under each line: F-C-G-D-A. This accompaniment (hereafter referred to as the "chord cycle" of the song) forms a kind of chaconne based on quadruple plagal motion: [$\flat$VI-$\flat$III | $\flat$VII-IV | I | I] . The relentlessness of the pattern emphasizes the essence of the drama: Joe's vengeance and flight are inexorable.

Along with the words and harmony, Roberts copyrighted a lead sheet for the first verse (Ex. 3). The tune consists of a four-note stepwise descent (A-G-F$^\sharp$-E), interrupted by a D in the second measure. As given in the lead sheet, however, the notes do not match the syllables of the verse written underneath them. In subsequent verses the number of syllables varies widely—how should one attach the notes to them? As in many folk songs, the uneven rhythms of the text probably should prompt the singer to vary the melody—using the four-note descent as a skeletal structure to be embellished. In other words, Roberts seems to have meant the "tune" of "Hey Joe" to be a general shape.

Several things about this "Hey Joe" have led people to question whether Roberts really wrote it. Because it draws on so many well-established song conventions, the song seems considerably older than the date of the copyright. And some observers claim that Roberts has not been consistent in explaining how he wrote the song. In his most fanciful account (according to his publisher), Roberts claims that the words came to him as he walked with a young woman along an East Coast beach. He wrote the words in the sand, but, of course, the tide washed them away. It was also the last time he saw the woman, his only witness to the occasion.[11] Others have claimed that it was a young woman who wrote the song; she died and Roberts claimed it.[12] To understand why the authorship of this "Hey

Example 3. The Original Lead Sheet for "Hey Joe," 1962

cont. from Music sheet.

No. 2. Going down town, buy me a Forty Four (44).
Repeat.
When I get through that woman won't run No more.

No. 3. Hey Joe, what are you gonna do?
Repeat.
Take my pistol, and Kill her before I'm through.

No. 4. Hey Joe, I heard you shot your woman dead.
Repeat.   or Smack Through the Head.
Yes I did; got both of them lying in that bed

No. 5. Hey Joe where do you think you'll go.
Repeat.
Leaving here think I'll go to Mexico.

No. 6. Yes I'm going, going where I can be free.
Repeat.
'Cause ain't No Hang man gonna put No
Noose on me.

William M. Roberts

Joe" seems so clouded, one must understand something of the time and place from which it emerged.

A gathering place for New York bohemians since the 1930s, Greenwich Village in 1962 was home to dozens of coffee houses, theaters, and bars where one could hear folk music. The cool jazz concerts and Beat poetry readings of the 1950s had more or less given way to weekly "hootenannies" (or "hoots") where dozens of folk musicians performed in a single night. As Happy Traum recalls, "On one hoot night there would be some fifty singer-songwriters playing their new tunes and another fifty singer-interpreters copying down the lyrics."[13] New songs spread rapidly through the community, partly because performers "borrowed" songs without crediting their authors. But, as one artist put it, it was also "a time of real generosity and sharing. . . . There was a lot of trading songs and teaching going back and forth."[14] In the process, songs often lost their provenance. Sylvia Tyson recalls Bob Dylan coming up to her and saying: "I just wrote a new song. At least, I think I wrote it. I might have heard it somewhere."[15] Traum recalls that, "After a while, the songs were more quickly recognized than the authors who penned them."[16] "Hey Joe" was probably one of those songs. How much of the song Roberts may or may not have picked up in the Village will probably never be known. But Roberts remains adamant that he wrote it and has "the copyright to prove it. To perpetuate speculation otherwise seems pointless."[17]

In any case, it was a Village singer-songwriter who brought the song to the attention of the world. Dino Valenti (born Chester Arthur Powers Jr.) began playing Village cafes and bars in about 1960. Considered by at least one Village observer as "talented beyond detail," Valenti became fairly well known for his aggressive guitar style and large appetite for methamphetamines.[18] By summer 1963 Valenti had left the Village and moved into a beached ferryboat in Sausalito, California, north of San Francisco. After playing as a solo artist in Bay Area clubs, he co-founded the group Quicksilver Messenger Service in 1965. But several weeks before the group's first scheduled performance the police arrested and jailed Valenti for possession of illegal drugs. To raise money for his defense he shopped around a tape of songs he hoped to sell—including "Hey Joe." Third Story Music bought the song and copyrighted it (with Valenti credited as author) in October 1965.

Third Story wanted the song because by then several bands were playing it, including one of the best-known groups in Los Angeles, the Byrds. They had gotten the song from their co-founder David Crosby—who, as it turned out, had learned it from Valenti when the two men roomed together on the Sausalito ferryboat. As the Byrds gained local fame, so did "Hey Joe." Soon other Los Angeles-based groups added "Hey Joe" to their repertoire. Bryan Maclean, the road manager for the Byrds, taught it to John Beck, the lead singer for the Leaves. Soon thereafter, Maclean joined Arthur Lee's group the Grassroots, who then changed their name to Love. The Leaves, Love, and other local groups realized the song's hit potential when fans started to request "Hey Joe" more than any other song.[19]

When the Byrds signed with Columbia Records in the spring of 1965, Crosby hoped they would include "Hey Joe" on their first album. But they did not. This left the Leaves, Love, and other groups in a quandary: who should record it, if not the Byrds? Crosby was said to be possessive about the song, feeling that he had "discovered" it. But local groups wondered if the song's omission from the Byrds' first album made it fair game for someone else to record.

The first group to record "Hey Joe" was apparently the Surfaris, who were best known for surf songs, including "Surfer Joe" (1962). They recorded "Hey Joe" in September 1965, but, perhaps out of loyalty to Crosby and the Byrds, did not include it on their November 1965 folk rock album, *It Ain't Me Babe*. This unreleased recording could not have influenced other groups. But it probably does reflect how some groups treated the song in those early days in Los Angeles. Indeed, three elements of the Surfaris' recording characterize many subsequent recordings of "Hey Joe": the structure of the text, the nature of the vocal delivery, and the guitar riff.

The Surfaris begin the text in the way most groups later would: they do not ask Joe where he is going with all that *money* in his hand, but with that *gun* in his hand. Joe replies that he is going to shoot his woman because of her cheating. The following verse asks Joe what he is going to do— an obvious redundancy, since Joe has just said what he is going to do. That redundancy, however, provokes the reply, "I guess I'll shoot 'em both before I'm through." Then, typical of many versions of the song, the Surfaris play an instrumental break after Joe's threat to kill—a lead guitar solo played over six chord cycles—symbolizing the passage of time as Joe carries out his threat. In this recording, however, unlike most later ones, Joe says nothing about Mexico. Instead he vows to go "where all those grass roots grow . . . where all those men are free, [where there] ain't nobody waitin' to stick me up in a big old tree."[20]

The Surfaris begin their version with a twelve-string guitar riff apparently adapted from the riff to "Needles and Pins" (written by Sonny Bono and Jack Nitzsche, a major hit for the British group the Searchers, 1964; see Ex. 4).[21] This riff exploits the left-hand fingering of an A chord on the

*In "Hey Joe" the D is often replaced by a C# and
the rhythm of this measure changed to:

Example 4. The "Needles and Pins" Guitar Riff

guitar in a way countless folk guitarists had previously done: the third
finger could be lifted up, exposing the open B string, then hammered back
down to give the C♯; or, the fourth finger added to give a D that, when the
finger is lifted, resolves back to the C♯. In some form or another, this riff
would appear in most subsequent versions of "Hey Joe."

In the fall of 1965 the Leaves were also anxious to record "Hey Joe."
John Beck explains: "What happened was some other bands started getting wise to [the song] and doing it and then I heard that Cory Wells and
the Enemies were going to record the song, which really pissed me off
because they weren't entitled to it at all—I mean, they just copied it from
all the rest of us. . . . We were smart enough to know that whoever put it
out first was going to have a hit record with it."[22] So in a (now disputed)
telephone conversation with Jim Dickson of the Byrds, Beck claims he got
the Byrds' permission to record "Hey Joe." The Leaves released a single
entitled "Hey, Joe, Where You Gonna Go?" in November 1965.

This recording of "Hey Joe" resembles the Surfaris' version in most
respects. The structure of the text and music closely resemble the Surfaris':
introduction, two verses, instrumental break, final verse, close.[23] A few
differences set it apart. One is the reference in the final verse to Mexico,
which was missing in the Surfaris' version. Another is the tempo. The
Surfaris played at a moderate tempo, luxuriating in the resonance of the
twelve-string guitar. Using only a six-string guitar with considerably less
resonance, the Leaves accelerate the pace of the strumming and hit the
strings harder for a more percussive effect. More than anything else, the
bass line distinguishes this version of "Hey Joe." Here bassist Jim Pons
creates a line that seems to drive upward as the harmony seems to fall. He
does this by arpeggiating the members of the first two triads and then
playing the line again a whole step higher (Ex. 5).

Example 5. Jim Pons's Bass Line under "Hey Joe" Chord Cycle

The Leaves' first recording of "Hey Joe" failed to reach anything but a small regional audience. The publishing arm of the Leaves' record company, however, copyrighted the song that December—attributing words and music to John Beck.

Determined to have a hit record with "Hey Joe," the Leaves recorded it again with a new guitarist in April 1966.[24] In this version they maintain the text and overall form of their earlier recording, but with one radical change. Instead of playing repetitions of the chord cycle between the second and third verses, they play a common rock 'n' roll-based bridge section as an instrumental break [IV | IV | I | I | IV | IV | V/V | V], performing it in the style of surf groups.[25] The Leaves also add two effects that increase the sense of power and menace in the song: a prominent fuzztone guitar and a shrieking lead guitar line on the first chord cycle. These modifications, in addition to a growing underground fascination with the song, helped make the Leaves' second version of "Hey Joe" a Top-40 hit in the spring of 1966.[26]

In the wake of the Leaves' success, two other prominent Los Angeles groups rushed to record the song. The Enemies issued a version that resembled the Surfaris and (first) Leaves versions, except that singer Cory Wells tried to characterize the two speakers in the song: he sings Joe's answers a full octave below the questions.[27] The Standells issued a version (titled "Hey Joe, Where You Gonna Go?") that amalgamates the earlier versions of the song. Lead singer Dick Dodd imitates John Beck's inflections, but also characterizes the dialogue's two speakers, as Cory Wells had. Dodd also returns to the Surfaris' version of Joe's destination—"down where the grass roots grow." Dodd adds that there "all you can do is dream"; but he makes no mention of the threat of hanging. Most distinctive about the Standells' version is the fade-out at the ending. Although seldom used by subsequent groups, the fade concludes the song successfully; it connotes the unending nature of the saga, the timelessness of the archetypal Joe.

Having been preempted by other groups, the Byrds finally issued their own version of "Hey Joe" as a track on their third album *5D (Fifth Dimen-*

sion) (1966). This version, sung by Crosby above agitated guitar strums, lacks the common embellishments of other versions: it has no "Needles and Pins" riff and no distinctive bass line. Crosby also follows Roberts's original lyrics closely. He asks Joe where he's going with all that *money* in his hand; Joe replies confusedly that he is going to find his woman; Joe then says he's going downtown to buy a "blue steel 44"; the narrator tells him "I heard you shot your woman dead"; Joe replies that he did because "I found them both in the same damn bed"; and so forth. Although the last verse uses the standard lines about Mexico, freedom, and the hangman, Crosby rounds off the lyrics by asking Joe again where he's going with all that money—suggesting, perhaps, the cyclical nature of vengeance. Like the Standells, the Byrds end the song with a fade.

After the Byrds released *5D,* Love released a single of "Hey Joe," a version that closely follows the Byrds' in its structure. Nevertheless, Love member Bryan MacLean complained that the Leaves had "stolen" *his* arrangement of the song—a complaint hard to accept, since so much disparity exists between the two groups' recordings of the song.[28] Also, the bass line of the Love recording sounds identical to the Surfaris', since Ken Forssi was the bassist for both.

Groups around the country began recording cover versions of the Los Angeles-based recordings of "Hey Joe." Most of them understandably imitate the Leaves' hit version. But most also vary the text in distinctive ways, as in the Hazards' version: Joe threatens to do something unintelligible to his woman's "feet" because "she's been runnin' out on me." A few groups even twisted the music—most flagrantly the Tempos, who unaccountably changed the chord cycle into a series of *ascending fourths* beginning on the tonic: [I-IV | ♭VII-♭III | I | I].[29] Other groups imitated the Byrds' version instead of the Leaves'. Most added little new or distinctive—consider for example the versions by the Heywoods, Euphoria's Id, Spirit, and the Litter.[30] Some groups added simple novelties to "psychedelicize" the song. The Cryan' Shames, for example, not only begin and end the song with the sound of a gong (panned across the stereo channels), but also play a modal contrapuntal duo between guitar and bass before starting the song in earnest. (To see how these devices connote "psychedelic" technique, see the discussion in the next chapter.) A few other groups elaborated in more substantial ways on the Byrds version.

Four of the most unusual of these deserve mention by name: the recordings of "Hey Joe" by the Warlocks, the Shadows of Knight, the Swamp Rats, and the Rogues. In the Warlocks' version, just after Joe vows to shoot his woman and her lover, gunshots fire, and an actor yells "You've done it for the last time, baby!" An actress screams and cries, more gunshots ensue, and a standard instrumental break follows. The Shadows of Knight recording of "Hey Joe" includes two instrumental breaks, the second of which consists of a long, one-chord rave-up derived from the Yardbirds' "I'm a Man." The rave-up contains a strange lead guitar solo on a harmonic minor scale; but during the last verse, when Joe announces he is going to Mexico, the harmonic minor solo resumes and is now clearly understood as a reference to flamenco music (which often uses that scale). The Swamp Rats completely change the text of "Hey Joe": the question-answer format is gone and Joe never speaks. The narrator not only perceives everything Joe is plotting, but also vows to execute vengeance on Joe's deeds:

> Hey Joe, I know what you're gonna do
> You think you can get away, but no, I'm gonna find you.
>
> Hey Joe, I'm gonna find you someday.
> When I do I know I'm gonna make you pay.

These and similar threats occupy the entire song. Finally, the Rogues rename the song "Wanted Dead or Alive," add a Bo Diddley riff (to the instrumental break) and recast the text as a monologue by Joe's intended victim. The refrain of this version becomes "I know what you're doin' with that gun / I know why you've got me on the run."

In the next several years, "Hey Joe" became an international hit. In the inevitable Mexican version, Los Locos del Ritmo sing it in Spanish. In most countries, however, non-English-speaking groups sang "Hey Joe" in English—as best they could. A Danish group, for example, unwittingly embellishes the text by filtering it through decidedly thick accents: they persistently sing "Hey Jue," ask questions about the "mahney" in his hand, and so on.[31] A Japanese group called the Golden Cups recorded a version of "Hey Joe" that adapts the song to different cultural standards:

> Hey Joe, where you gonna go?
> Goin' downtown, gonna buy me a gun.
>
> Hey Joe, where you goin' with that gun in your hand?
> Gonna shoot this guy, well, he's been flirtin' with my girlfriend.

These two brief interchanges, uttered at the song's beginning and ending, comprise the entire text.[32]

After the first recordings of "Hey Joe," Third Story Music published the song. The sheet music pitches the song in D—not in the A that Roberts and subsequent artists had used. The printed melody follows the scalewise descent most singers preferred (now transposed to D-C-B♭-A). The accompaniment includes the "Needles and Pins" riff but omits the walking bass line of the Leaves and others. The sheet music lacks an instrumental bridge. But the lyrics begin, "Hey Joe, where ya goin' with that gun in your hand"—not "that money"—and goes on to follow the Leaves' version of the text.

Third Story initially paid royalties to Valenti. Meanwhile, Billy Roberts, who was fronting his own group, the Billy Moses Blues Bag, "made no secret of the fact that he wrote 'Hey Joe.'"[33] After the publication of the song, a friend of Roberts's confronted Third Story, who in turn confronted Valenti. Valenti admitted he had not written the song, but simply "picked it up." Roberts's agent arranged to have Third Story continue publishing "Hey Joe," now crediting (and paying) Roberts.[34]

After almost losing out on the royalties to a hit song, Roberts began a copyrighting spree. Before 1966 he had copyrighted only two songs, "Hey Joe" and "Woman on the Way." But during 1966 he copyrighted eleven more; in the next few years he copyrighted dozens more (including one called "Hey Rube"). Although he sold some of these songs, none of them has yet become a hit.

*

Tim Rose was another Greenwich Village singer, a gravelly voiced twelve-string guitarist with a distinct personal aesthetic: "There are only two kinds of songs. Songs about getting laid and songs about not getting laid. That's what music's all about."[35] "Hey Joe" fit that aesthetic rather well; Rose recorded it in New York in April 1966—one month before the Leaves' version entered the charts.

Entitled "Hey Joe (You Shot Your Woman Down)" the recording differs completely from the Leaves'. Rose plays the song at less than half the tempo. He changes the key of the song to E and begins it not with the "Needles and Pins" riff, but with a distinctive blues-based guitar lick. By placing the song in E (instead of A), Rose was able to play guitar figurations that completely differed from West-Coast versions of the song.[36] Rose roars out the verses, and adds his own variant on their structure. Several other versions had said "I heard you shot your woman dead," to which Joe replied that he did, "just like I said," or because he had found them "in the same damn bed." Rose changes the line to "I heard you shot your woman *down*"; Joe then replies that he did it because he "caught [her] out runnin' around," then shouts "so I shot her!" Following that line, Rose adds a chorus, strings, and deep artificial reverberation. These latter elements heighten the drama of the song, seemingly elevating it to a tragedy, not so much composed as handed down through generations. The song credit on the record seems to say as much: it contains only the statement "Arranged and Adapted by Tim Rose."

Rose's version never entered the national charts, although in the fall of 1966 it did become a minor hit in some areas of California. But the record did inspire several groups and artists around the country to record it Rose's way (the Chosen Few and the Velvet Hammer, for example).[37] The most important cover of Rose's "Hey Joe" came from a then little-known artist named Jimi Hendrix.

Hendrix had grown up in the Pacific Northwest, the garage rock mecca of the 1960s. In 1965 Hendrix formed his own band, Jimmy James and the Blue Flames, with whom he began playing "Hey Joe" in 1966.[38] Hendrix probably learned the song from his friend Arthur Lee (of Love), but later stated his belief that the song was not a new one: "'Hey Joe' is a traditional song and it's about 100 years old." Explaining that "lots of people have done different arrangements of it" and that "there are probably 1,000 versions of it fast," Hendrix credited Tim Rose as the first to do it slowly, the way he preferred.[39] That is how he recorded the song in November 1966, intending it to be the first single by his new group, the Jimi Hendrix Experience. Decca rejected it, undoubtedly wondering why yet another version of "Hey Joe" was necessary, but Polydor agreed to release it. The record became a Top-10 hit in the United Kingdom.

Hendrix's version—credited on the label as "traditional, arr. Jimi Hendrix"—mimics Rose's in many respects, including text, key, tempo, opening guitar riff, choral backing, heavy reverberation, and dramatic sweep. Hendrix also embellishes the text with phrases rooted in rhythm and blues. He refers to Joe's woman as his "old lady," adds extra rhymes ("shot her down, shot her down to the ground now"), and spontaneously interjects comments like "dig," and "that ain't too cool." Moreover, he transforms Jim Pons's sequential bass line into a guitar+bass melodic riff that resembles those of Motown bassist James Jamerson: instead of arpeggiating the triads up, he sometimes begins on the root of a triad then leaps *down* to its third and completes the chord by moving in half steps (Ex. 6). In some ways, this record tread the line between garage rock and psyche-

Example 6. Noel Redding's Bass Line under "Hey Joe" Chord Cycle. Redding plays the song in E major; his bass line is transposed here to the original key of A for ease of comparison.

delic music. Hendrix's "Hey Joe" was "garage" in its loose, let's-try-it attitude, its fuzzy guitar doubling the bass line, and its decidedly unsingerly vocal. But it was "psychedelic" in its slow, reverberant unfolding and jazz-influenced guitar lines (traits we will discuss more in the next chapter).

Within a few months of releasing "Hey Joe," Hendrix became a star in the United States. Although he never released "Hey Joe" as a single in the United States, his album *Are You Experienced?* which contained "Hey Joe," reached Number 5 on the charts. Two singers tried to capitalize on Hendrix's success by recording singles that faithfully covered his version of "Hey Joe"; both covers made the national charts. The first cover, released in the summer of 1967, was by Cher (then half of Sonny and Cher). She sings the song in the original key of A, but copies as best she can all of Hendrix's textual idiosyncrasies and mannerisms. Behind her voice, strings play and a choir sings, while the bassist plays incessantly the bass line Noel Redding (of Hendrix's group) had played only sparingly. The second cover of Hendrix's "Hey Joe" was a straightforward slow soul arrangement by Wilson Pickett, replete with a horn section, tambourines, a heavy backbeat, and a gospel-derived vocal. This arrangement, released in summer of 1970, places the song squarely in the rhythm-and-blues vocal tradition that Hendrix had evoked in his arrangement. The recording changes "Hey Joe" into full-fledged "soul music," an idiom where, indeed, songs about obsessive relationships seemed to flourish.

Hendrix's British success with the song led some British groups to record it. The most notable was Deep Purple. Their version, more than seven and a half minutes long, begins with a recording of a police siren, overlaid with an organ playing flamenco riffs in E over quasi-Mexican dance rhythms (such as the bolero). The sectional introduction builds in intensity for two minutes and fifteen seconds before the familiar chord cycle begins—in E major with virtually all the riffs, fills, and textual anomalies of Hendrix's. After the words "I shot her!" the group resumes the pseudo bolero, then returns to the chord cycle with a Hendrix-like guitar solo. And like Hendrix, Deep Purple believed the song was in the public domain. Unlike Hendrix, they took credit for it outright, attributing "Hey Joe" simply to "Deep Purple."

In the ensuing years Hendrix's became the standard, almost definitive version of "Hey Joe." Now, virtually all published versions of the song use not only Hendrix's version of the text, but every detail of his delivery of the melody. In the meantime, Tim Rose's "Hey Joe" became a historical footnote, merely a precursor to Hendrix's version.

Nevertheless, in its day, Rose's arrangement of the song strongly affected how many other groups would perceive "Hey Joe." His slow, introspective treatment made the song an apt vehicle for early forms of psychedelic rock and heavy metal, with all of the pretense and seriousness found in those genres. His radical reduction of tempo made the song less dependent on the raucous energy and instrumental busywork of earlier versions.[40] It also allowed the singer to interject more ideas into the spaces between verses. In one case, the result was what appears to be the first gay version of the song. Near the end of the recording by Group Therapy (1968), the (male) lead singer follows successive statements of the words "Hey Joe" with a series of exclamations including: "I need you," "Don't leave me!" and finally, "I love you!"

The meditativeness of Rose's version suggested to some artists that "Hey Joe" could be rewritten, changed from a crime ballad into a reflective, almost philosophical song. In November 1966, just after Rose's version hit the regional charts, the Los Angeles-based Music Machine recorded its own slow version. Lead singer Sean Bonniwell had first heard the song in 1962 at a folk club in Hermosa Beach, California. "I knew it was too fast the minute I heard it," he recalls, and he unsuccessfully tried to get his folk trio, the Wayfarers, to mount a slower version. Years later he heard Tim Rose perform the song and convinced his new group, the Music Machine, to do a similar arrangement, including some fresh lyrics he had written.[41] In Bonniwell's version, Joe threatens to kill his woman but never actually does it. Instead, Bonniwell sings, "Hey Joe, do you think you'll ever die?" Joe responds, quizzically, "I don't believe in money, fortune, fame—all dirty lies." He then says he will go to Mexico, after which the narrator takes over the rest of the song with commentary on the subject of death: "Hey Joe, you can't die until your time [because] death is the glove that fits the hands of time." He then laments tersely that "it's too soon, too soon" to die.

The Music Machine's version directly influenced several other groups. At least one, the Frantic, imitated it note for note. Another, Fever Tree, actually combined a Music Machine-like "Hey Joe" with a Leaves-like fast version. In their 1969 recording, Fever Tree plays the Music Machine's slow version verbatim (in F♯), then changes the key (to A) and gradually accelerates the music to reach the tempo of the Leaves' version. The group then plays the latter in its entirety (including the surf-music bridge), modulates back to F♯ and resumes the Music Machine version—again, playing the whole song. The result is a track more than twelve minutes long.[42]

For his first "psychedelic" album, Johnny Rivers followed the Rose/Hendrix model of "Hey Joe," but completely rewrote the lyrics. In Rivers' version the narrator asks Joe a series of searching questions about his destiny.

> Hey Joe, where are you goin' with your eyes closed?
> Can't you tell you're goin' any way the wind blows?
>
> Hey Joe, tell me where are you goin' to run to?
> Makes no difference, Joe, they're gonna find you.
>
> Hey Joe, will you search your whole life through
> Just to find the truth right inside you?
>
> Hey Joe, tell me what are you gonna do?
> If you know yourself they just can't find you.

The questions are all rhetorical—Joe is never allowed to respond.

It was probably inevitable that some artists would spoof "Hey Joe." Frank Zappa and the Mothers of Invention use the question-answer format and chord progression of "Hey Joe" as the basis for "Flower Punk" (1967), a satire of the "flower power" culture centered in San Francisco. It begins: "Hey Punk, where you goin' with that flower in your hand? / Well, I'm goin' up to Frisco to join a psychedelic band." The narrator goes on to ask "Punk" where he's going with various aspects of hippie attire (hair, beads, button), prompting naive answers about going to a love-in, to a dance, and finally, to a "shrink so he can help me be a nervous wreck." A year later, the Arbors released a version that parodied the exaggerated vocal style of early incarnations of "Hey Joe." As the singer strains to go into his upper range, he sings,

> Hey Joe, got me higher than before—
> Don't you know [I] can't take those sounds no more.
>
> Hey Joe, [straining] I can't make it up that high.
> No Joe, don't make me try.

The text draws to a close with the question, "Hey Joe, where you goin' with that woodchuck in your hand?"

Perhaps the strangest reworking of "Hey Joe" was the recording by Mad Sound entitled "To Masturbate" (1967?).[43] The music is unmistakably that of "Hey Joe," but the singing is so garbled as to make it unintelligible—except for some vague allusions to self-gratification.

Nothing showed more convincingly that "Hey Joe" had become a standard than the recording by King Curtis in 1969: it was an *instrumental* version. Since the text is not sung and the song itself has no fixed melody, virtually nothing remains to identify "Hey Joe" but the title and the chord cycle. But while Curtis uses the chord cycle as little more than a backdrop to saxophone improvisation, the recording is instantly recognizable as an arrangement of "Hey Joe." Playing in Hendrix's key and tempo, Curtis proceeds through the chord cycle four times, then inserts a twelve-bar blues progression (with funk drumming behind it) in the key of A. Two more chord cycles follow, then two extra measures of an E chord, followed by the twelve-bar bridge. The chord cycle resumes and the record fades.

*

Perhaps the test of any purported standard is whether it can survive its own popularity: will a new generation of performers still want to invest the energy to learn something that might seem dated or outmoded? "Hey Joe" did survive into the 1970s and beyond, thanks largely to Patti Smith, one of the early exponents of garage rock's next generation, now known as "punk." In her first single, entitled "Hey Joe (Version)" (1974), Smith revamps the song into a tribute to Patty Hearst (the heiress who had been kidnapped by the Symbionese Liberation Army, then joined them in a bank robbery and became a fugitive). Smith opens the record by reciting a poem in which she asks Hearst, "Now that you're on the run, what goes on in your mind?" She goes on to speak in the voice of Hearst's father: "Sixty days ago, she was such a lovely child. Now here she is with a gun in her hand." The opening chords of "Hey Joe" ensue. Smith sings the song with phrases taken from Hendrix's version—"old lady," "that ain't cool," "I gave her the gun," "shoot her one more time for me"—but reshapes the melody into something far more disjunct than it had ever been. After she sings about going to Mexico, Smith transforms the voice of Joe into the voice of Patty Hearst (referring to a widely published photo of the heiress in military garb and stance): "when I was standin' there under that flag with a carbine between my legs you know I felt so free. They can run me down like a dog and I will stay on the run. . . . Daddy, you'll never know just what I was feelin' . . . I'm no pretty little rich girl, I'm nobody's million-dollar baby, I'm nobody's patsy anymore, I feel so free."

Smith's version took "Hey Joe" as a kind of *objet trouvé,* a household object upon which one could layer new ideas and paradigms. While no one since has been so audacious as Smith in revising "Hey Joe," her version signaled the birth of the new progeny of "Hey Joe." Since Smith's recording, artists consistently revise the song and hybridize it with other styles: Jerry Douglas presents "Hey Joe" as a virtuoso bluegrass song (1992); Willy DeVille performs it with mariachi horns (1994); Buckwheat Zydeco plays it as a cajun song; Bevis Frond plays it new wave; Black Uhuru plays it reggae.[44]

Of all the songs of its day, why did "Hey Joe" become an icon? For one thing, its text had just the right balance of elements (and the right lack of melody) to make it appeal not only to garage bands of the 1960s, but also to the punk bands who presided over much of the rock of the late 1970s and early 1980s. The song's lyrics displayed the sort of macho bravado, violent imagery, defiance, and alienation that garage bands reveled in: Joe carries a gun openly, shoots a woman who dares to cross him, and outwits the "system" to find personal freedom. The question-answer format of the narrative allowed singers to create distinct personae; the lack of a real melody seemed to free the song from vocal constraints, enabling post-Jagger singers to employ all of their mannerisms.

For another thing, the harmonic progression fit the guitar nicely; it was a post-"Gloria" multiple-plagal chord progression easily fingered on the instrument. Moreover, the progression never changed throughout the song—that made it easy—yet the harmonic rhythm was relatively swift— that made it sound more difficult. For groups accustomed to three-chord progressions the *five* chords of "Hey Joe" seemed harmonically rich indeed.

Finally, the mysteries of its origins made the song tantalizing. The multiple claims to authorship or the claim that the song was essentially authorless probably were the best things that could have happened to "Hey Joe." If in the mid-1960s one thought the song was *already* a standard (i.e., an old folk song), one would be inclined to play with it, changing the words, the tune, and the formal structure—there was no proprietor to whom one had to be true. And so the song proliferated, if for no other reason than this: almost no one believed it could be owned.

The appropriation of "Hey Joe" by, as Bangs said, "everybody and his . . . brother" was true to the ethos of the song: the freedom to do as one pleases is more important than the strictures of law, whether in defiance of the hangman or the copyright office. To claim to have written or discovered "Hey Joe" asserted something deep in the American character, a spirit of claim-staking, the notion of "finders, keepers." All of which made ironic the popularity of "Hey Joe." A song about obsessive jealousy ended up belonging to everyone—and, in the process, made Billy Roberts's copyright worth something after all.

5 Getting Psyched

In 1938 Swiss chemist Albert Hofmann derived his twenty-fifth drug from lysergic acid. He called it *Lyserg-säure-diäthylamid,* abbreviated it "LSD-25," tested the drug on animals, and reported it to be a mild stimulant. Five years later he accidentally ingested a tiny amount and experienced first-hand its powerful effects. It distorted his sense of time; long events seemed to pass in a flash and single moments became eternities.[1] The drug unloosed his sense of self, melting it into the environment. And everything in the room around him became fluid; the furniture appeared "in constant motion, animated, as if driven by an inner restlessness."[2]

In 1957 a New Jersey psychiatrist coined a word to describe these sensations: "psychedelic" (from the Greek for "mind-manifesting"). The term caught on. Within ten years it was a household term that people used to describe almost anything, from neo-expressionist paintings to strip shows. And soon an entire class of music came to be known by a pharmacological name.

To appreciate the importance of this music, one should understand how LSD-25 affected it. Some scholars question whether this can be done, whether one can connect with any specificity the drug's effects and the music's methods. A medical writer argues that "the psychopharmacological properties of the [hallucinogen] did not directly produce the musical forms."[3] Two musicologists suggest that "psychedelic" traits in the music do not depend on drugs: "The [psychedelic] system is perfectly structured internally [with] no necessary connection to anything outside itself."[4] Even Barry Melton of Country Joe and the Fish (a band often called psychedelic) takes the same point of view: "Drugs may have had a lot to do with the periphery . . . but not really a lot to do with the music itself."[5] But most rock musicians of the 1960s insisted then and continue to affirm that LSD-25—commonly known as "LSD" or "acid"—directly shaped their music. Psychedelic music, says one, was meant as "an LSD session without the use of drugs."[6] Another explains that LSD "opened you up to a whole new set of musical values."[7] When we see what those values are, we discover that "psychedelic" is in some ways the flip-side of "garage"—superficially different but inseparable.

*

As the 1950s closed, newspapers and magazines began to promote LSD as a new wonder drug. Two major articles set the tone. One, a feature article in *Look* magazine, glowingly recounted how LSD transformed actor Cary Grant, giving him the inner peace he had sought his whole life.[8] Another, in *This Week* magazine, explained that LSD "has rescued many drug addicts, alcoholics, and neurotics from their private hells—and holds promise for curing tomorrow's mental ills."[9] The public praise continued into the early 1960s, when two best-selling books and virtually every major magazine celebrated LSD as a psychotherapeutic miracle.[10]

In this period "LSD" made its first appearance in music. A surf group named the Gamblers issued a single entitled "Moon Dawg" in 1960; its B-side bore the title "LSD-25." The title had none of the connotations it might later have had.[11] The authors of the tune, Sam Taylor and Derry Weaver, read it in a magazine and thought it sounded good—like many other abbreviated high-tech titles adopted into surf music (e.g., the Majestics' "X-L3," the Tornados' "7-0-7," the What Four's "Gemini 4," the Challengers' "K-39," and Dick Dale and his Deltones' "My X-KE"). And like so many surf records, this B-side was a simple, passionately played instrumental in twelve-bar blues form. The title connoted nothing about the musical content, but only demonstrated that the name "LSD" was being assimilated into mass culture.

In 1964 the word "psychedelic" appeared for the first time on a record. The previous year a New York-based folk duo, the Holy Modal Rounders, recorded a version of Leadbelly's oft-covered "Hesitation Blues." Their version included this new final verse: "Got my psychedelic feet in my psychedelic shoes; / I believe, Lordy mama, I got the psychedelic blues."

When the record came out in early 1964, few understood the word "psychedelic." One folk artist who learned the song from the record rendered the word "cycle-belly," later realizing the mistake.[12]

In 1964, despite years of positive publicity, the tide of opinion about LSD turned. Newspaper reports blamed the drug for dangerous psychoses and accidental suicides. In late 1965 the federal government banned LSD distribution; Sandoz Laboratories, the drug's original maker, recalled all existing supplies. Nevertheless, in June 1966, psychiatrists announced at a national conference in Berkeley that they were "losing control" of LSD.[13] The drug had gone underground: people were producing it in kitchen labs and selling it as private entertainment.

In the fall of 1965, before the LSD ban went into effect, writer Ken Kesey and a few friends—the so-called "Merry Pranksters"—sponsored a series of "Acid Tests" in the San Francisco Bay Area. These were free-form symposia where the participants took LSD in order to enhance their experience of music, dance, experimental films, lighting effects, and recitations. One feature of the Acid Tests was the "Psychedelic Symphony," a name the Pranksters had used since 1964 for the performance of improvised LSD-oriented music. Anyone could and did perform in the "symphony," including members of the Grateful Dead, the house band of the Acid Tests. All instruments were welcome, but the ensemble regularly included an old Hammond organ and the Pranksters' "thunder machines," large noisemakers assembled from auto parts, piano strings, and the like. The result, according to Tom Wolfe, sounded like "atonal Chinese music."[14]

In January 1966, Kesey co-sponsored a sequel to the Acid Tests, a three-day event called the "Trips Festival."[15] It featured the usual mix of media, including slide projections, Native American dances, readings from Beatles songs, and music by the Grateful Dead, the Psychedelic Symphony, and the San Francisco Tape Center. The program for the festival called it "a new medium of communication & entertainment," adding that "maybe this is the ROCK REVOLUTION." The event proved so successful that its producer, Bill Graham, began a series of weekly sequels at the Fillmore Auditorium.

Graham's Fillmore shows and others like them throughout the Bay Area featured music by the Grateful Dead, Quicksilver Messenger Service, Jefferson Airplane, the Great Society, the Paul Butterfield Blues Band, Love, and the 13th Floor Elevators—a Texas-based band that in August 1966 issued the first rock album to call itself "psychedelic": *The Psychedelic Sounds of the 13th Floor Elevators*. Its liner notes unabashedly explained that the record celebrated the potential of man "to chemically alter his mental state[,] restructure his thinking and change his language."[16]

But the music on the record—like that of all the San Francisco groups—was not so much a new language as an amalgamation of dialects. Its fuzztone guitars and stereotypical chord progressions echoed garage rock; but its frequent minor keys, twangy guitars, and deep reverberation sounded like surf music. Although the group's lead singer sang with garage-rock aggression, the backing vocalists sang smoothly, like folk singers. The album's strangest special effect, a constant quavering hoot, was actually an amplified bluegrass jug. Most of the songs were a standard form and length (about three minutes); but "Roller Coaster" consisted of a five-minute, pseudo–Middle Eastern dirge in the aeolian mode.

The stylistic mix of the 13th Floor Elevators exemplified the "San Francisco sound," which, because of its context, became virtually synonymous with "psychedelic music." It was an eclectic style that a local underground newspaper called "the first head music we've had since the end of the Baroque."[17] This style derived largely from Beat culture folk music, since the local music scene was increasingly populated by singers who had emigrated from Greenwich Village in the early 1960s—Dino Valenti, for example, who had not only transplanted "Hey Joe" to the West Coast but had also brought civil-rights oriented songs like his own "Get Together" into the burgeoning hippie culture.[18] To this folk style were added the traces of garage rock and surf music mentioned above as well as influences from outside American popular music: Middle Eastern music (a commonplace in the international milieu of the San Francisco Bay Area), and certain jazz and classical music that had been influenced by it as well, particularly that of John Coltrane and Karlheinz Stockhausen.

In the early 1960s Coltrane had issued a series of exotic jazz albums, including *My Favorite Things* (1960), consisting of four long arrangements of showtunes, and *A Love Supreme* (1964), in which Coltrane developed all the material from a small chant motive. These records emphasized minor modes and long, organic improvisations modeled by Coltrane after the solo playing of sitar player Ravi Shankar.[19] Some of Coltrane's later, freer recordings derived largely from his own use of LSD, in which he claimed to perceive "the interrelationship of all life forms."[20] The rising generation of psychedelic musicians imitated Coltrane directly. In 1966 the Paul Butterfield Blues Band issued a thirteen-minute long pseudo-Coltrane track entitled "East-West." The Doors based the middle section of their 1966 song "Light My Fire" on Coltrane's version of "My Favorite Things."[21] The same year, in the Byrds' "Eight Miles High," Roger McGuinn played a solo guitar opening that not only imitated Coltrane's style but literally quoted the principal motive from Coltrane's "India."[22] James Gurley of Big Brother and the Holding Company explained: "I thought that if you could play guitar like John Coltrane played the sax, it would be really far out. That's what I was trying to do—of course nobody understood it, especially me."[23] Many other guitarists took on the veneer of Coltrane simply by emphasizing minor keys and modes—heretofore rare in rock 'n' roll, except for surf music instrumentals.

Internationally famed as an avant-garde electronic composer, Stockhausen had begun to draw on multicultural musics in his recent works. During the 1966–67 school year, as a visiting professor at U.C. Davis and guest of the San Francisco Tape Center, he became something of a local musical celebrity. In 1967 reviews of Stockhausen records appeared alongside reviews of rock records in the Bay Area-based *Rolling Stone* magazine. The juxtaposition suggests how beloved Stockhausen was among local rock players. Indeed, in assessing musical influences on the San Francisco sound, Darby Slick of the Great Society mentions Stockhausen in the same breath as Coltrane.[24] And rock musicians experienced his influence indirectly via the Stockhausen-inspired "A Day in the Life" on the Beatles' *Sgt. Pepper's Lonely Hearts Club Band* (1967).[25]

In the spring of 1966 British musicians had also begun to grapple with the influence of psychedelic drugs. In April the Pretty Things issued a record entitled "£.s.d."—a word-play on the British abbreviation for pounds (£.), schillings (s.), and pence (d.). The music was conventional rock and the lyrics alluded more to money than drugs. But the meaning of the shouted lyrics "I need L.S.D.!" was clear to the initiated. In October the Yardbirds' new single "Happenings Ten Years Time Ago" was promoted as "psychedelic"—fittingly, since the group had exploited minor keys, sitars, and Middle Eastern chant in their records since 1965. In December the Yardbirds recorded a brief, minimalistic instrumental entitled "L.S.D," but did not release it. As 1967 opened, the British rock newspaper *Melody Maker* invoked the term for the first time, applying it to two groups, Pink Floyd and the Move. Both of these groups played at free-form "happenings" and "freak-outs," events that, like Kesey's in San Francisco, mingled lighting effects, music, and spontaneous theater pieces. As it turned out, both groups rejected the term psychedelic as applied to their music. Pink Floyd explained that "there isn't really a definition for the word. . . . It's something that has all taken place around us—not within us." The Move was more blunt: "Psychedelic music is a load of _ _ _ _. . . . And we get quite nasty to anybody who calls us psychedelic." Of their recent single "Night of Fear" one group member remarked, "I'm instructed to say it's all about LSD but to tell you the truth, I haven't a bloody clue what it's all about."[26]

The Beatles' profoundly influential *Sgt. Pepper's Lonely Hearts Club Band* (released June 1967) contained the song "Lucy in the Sky with Diamonds," which many not surprisingly took as a reference to "LSD."[27] Upon the album's release, Paul McCartney indirectly promoted psychedelic music by publicly admitting he had taken LSD and that it had illuminated his music-making.[28] Several prominent British musicians quickly retorted; Graham Nash of the Hollies complained that "those who use the [hallucinogenic] stuff should know better. . . . It's doing a lot of harm to the entertainment industry."[29] Even McCartney's fellow band member George Harrison insisted that psychedelic drugs were only a crude method of achieving what could better be had through Eastern religious practices. "If you're really hip, you don't get involved with LSD," Harrison said in September 1967.[30] Nevertheless, the Beatles' music of that period seemed to demonstrate to the world the virtues of LSD-inspired music.

By late 1967 the word "psychedelic" already suffered from overuse. Virtually every rock band was calling itself—or allowing itself to be called—"psychedelic," no matter what the band's actual style or whether its members used drugs. An executive at Elektra Records worried that the word had become one which "will do for pop music what the hootenanny did for folk. I think it will ultimately destroy anything good that has been coming out of it."[31]

*

Now, in retrospect, how can "psychedelic" be a useful adjective for musical style and technique? Many groups that are generally considered "psychedelic" played in a variety of styles (example: the Doors); and many groups not generally considered psychedelic sometimes indulged in music that *is* considered psychedelic (example: Tommy James and the Shondells). To understand what makes music stylistically "psychedelic," one should consider three fundamental effects of LSD: dechronicization, depersonalization, and dynamization. *Dechronicization* permits the drug user to move outside of conventional perceptions of time. *Depersonalization* allows the user to lose the self and gain an "awareness of undifferentiated unity."[32] *Dynamization,* as Leary wrote, makes everything from floors to lamps seem to bend, as "familiar forms dissolve into moving, dancing structures";[33] objects become liquid, "dripping, streaming, with white-hot light or electricity," as though the "substance and form" of the world were "still molten."[34] Music that is truly "psychedelic" mimics these three effects.

On the simplest level, dechronicization lengthens songs and slows them down. Psychedelic groups retarded the beat, a practice easily perceived in cover versions. Vanilla Fudge's 1967 remake of the Supremes' "You Keep Me Hanging On" is typical; it converts the Motown tempo of ♩ = 128 to a relatively ponderous ♩ = 85. That kind of slowing could in itself dramatically lengthen a song. But psychedelic musicians often went further, attaching long instrumental introductions and codas or inserting long solos or "jams." That is, they treated a rock song like a jazz chart, a starting place for a series of improvisations that explored the implications of the basic material. Thus, the beat in Quicksilver Messenger Service's recording of Bo Diddley's "Who Do You Love" is slightly slower than that of the original; yet their version lasts twenty-five minutes—more than ten times the length of the original.

There were also practical reasons for psychedelic groups to slow and lengthen their songs. Jerry Garcia of the Grateful Dead recalls that "a lot of the early [psychedelic] bands were just a collection of friends, some of whom could play instruments, some of whom couldn't."[35] The technical deficiencies fostered expansive, open-ended forms. Darby Slick puts it bluntly: "At first, all we *could* play was free-form jams."[36] Many groups, even when they knew actual songs, seldom knew enough of them to play a full set unless they lengthened them. That had been the case with the Yardbirds, according to drummer Jim McCarty: "We used to play these all-nighters, sometimes three hours a night and we didn't have that much material. So we used to spread it all out and do these tempo changes and go into long free-form passages just to make the numbers longer."[37] Similarly, Iron Butterfly guitarist Erik Braunn recalls that they kept lengthening their psychedelic anthem "In-A-Gadda-Da-Vida" "because we didn't have enough material for a whole set."[38] When recorded, the song lasted over seventeen minutes.

The substance of what was being played also fostered dechronicization. In music one experiences the passage of time largely according to the disposition of musical events; quasi-hypnotic repetition and the absence of musical goals change the sense of time-passage dramatically. Many lead guitarists in psychedelic bands improvised in chain-link fashion, repeating ideas immediately, but varying the end of the idea in order to lead into a new idea, and so on. Beneath such non-directional solos, bassists often played ostinatos. The undirected solos and endless ostinatos led the listener into what Jonathan Kramer calls "vertical time," a near stasis in which change and anticipation are minimal.[39]

Groups could depersonalize their music by changing their idea of ensemble—which in turn changed the musical texture. Heretofore, a player in a rock group assumed the role either of lead player or accompanimental player, foreground or background. But psychedelic drugs, as one musician said, "allowed you to get together as a group without being competitive."[40] That lack of instrumental competition made LSD-oriented groups emulate the textures of free jazz, which sometimes approached a kind of "democratic counterpoint."[41] In 1966 Jerry Slick described succinctly the new psychedelic ideal of texture: "We've got too many people playing the same notes in the same range with the same rhythm. If we can play more like counter-point, and in different ranges, our sound'll get a lot bigger."[42]

But psychedelic musicians depersonalized in a more profound way, by turning up their volume and drenching their sound in artificial reverberation. One user said that on LSD, "I suddenly 'knew' what it was to be simultaneously a guitar, the sounds, the ear that received them, and the organism that responded."[43] Some bands imitated that effect by dissolving the barrier between music and listener: they played through stacks of amplifiers at extraordinarily high levels, making listeners feel the vibrations of their instruments instead of just hearing them. (This was especially striking to folk-music oriented listeners, who scarcely had heard music through amplifiers at all before.) The result was, in Sheila Whiteley's words, a "drowning of individual consciousness."[44]

Yet hallucinogens also often made sounds seem far away. One user described the depersonalizing effect of that: "You hear the music [as if] way down in a cavern, and suddenly it is you who is way down in the cavern. Are you now the music, or is the music now at the mouth of the cavern? Did you change places with it? and so on?"[45] Mimicking this LSD effect, psychedelic groups used huge amounts of electronic reverberation (previously associated with surf music) or simply recorded in the halls where they usually performed—the Fillmore Auditorium, for example. In surf music the artificial reverberation had connoted vast, overwhelming oceanic spaces.[46] In psychedelic music the reverberation suggested enormous interior spaces. When groups both turned up the volume and added reverberation, they made the music sound both closer and farther away at the same time. Which is precisely the sort of depersonalizing paradox that some Native Americans described in their use of hallucinogens: "That which sounds far away . . . [also] sounds as if it were very near."[47]

More than anything else, psychedelic music dynamized musical parameters previously stable in rock. Psychedelic drugs transformed fixed shapes into shifting shapes. In turn, psychedelic rock activated the music's essential form, harmony, timbre, articulation, and spatial deployment.

Rock 'n' roll musicians generally used simple, well-established forms, most commonly twelve-bar blues or thirty-two-bar song form (i.e., two verses = 16, bridge = 8, return of verse = 8). The music, generally dance-based, tended to sound uniform—it denoted contrasting sections with new chords and drum patterns, but not with new tempi or drastically different styles. By the mid-1960s, however, some groups expanded the bridge section of the form into a truly contrasting one. In 1965, for example, the Yardbirds released "For Your Love," whose bridge differs completely in instrumentation, tempo, and texture from the opening and closing sections. Meanwhile, Frank Zappa and the Mothers of Invention recorded a song in 1965, "Help, I'm a Rock," which actually includes at least four movements, one of which is reprised in the album's following song, "The Return of the Son of Monster Magnet." Neither the Yardbirds nor the Mothers referred to psychedelic drugs in these recordings, but many listeners assumed as much from the title of the Mothers album—*Freak Out.*

Some San Francisco-based groups continued the elaboration of form, making multi-movement songs and changing their beat divisions and tempi from section to section. For instance, in their instrumental entitled "Section 43" (1966), Country Joe and the Fish juxtapose three discrete sections, each joined by a pause or a held organ chord: the A section, containing a moderate-speed guitar melody in 4/4, moves abruptly to a B section in a much slower, compound meter; the brief C section is a transitional, quasi-music hall guitar riff. The overall form is A-B-A^1-C-A^2-B^1.[48]

Groups as diverse as the Beatles, the Mothers, and Quicksilver Messenger Service did similarly. They segued individual songs in such a way as to make a whole album side become a single track; in concert they played successive songs *attacca,* without pausing from one to the next. Many lesser-known groups followed suit, realizing that a band could "psychedelicize" a song at the macro level by simply juxtaposing disparate sonic blocks. Recordings from 1967 by groups such as Teddy and His Patches, Bohemian

Vendetta, Opal Butterfly, and the Bougalieu contain songs that juxtapose widely contrasting sections or that insert foreign passages into otherwise consistent songs. Even the mainstream group the Buckinghams released a routine pop song named "Susan" (1967) into which the producer, James Guercio, inserted thirty seconds of orchestral sound mass and collage.[49]

*

Some artists dynamized their harmony by adding chromatic neighbor, appoggiatura, and passing chords. Several groups embellished the tonic chord of a song with the Neapolitan chord (♭II) as an upper neighbor, adapting the jazz technique called "side slipping" (sliding the "real" harmony up or down a half step and then back).[50] Thus, Jefferson Airplane's "House at Pooneil Corners" (1968) consists almost entirely of an oscillation between i and ♭II.[51] Some also used the Neapolitan as an appoggiatura to the tonic—as in the Great Society's "Arbitration" (1966), the Doors' "The Crystal Ship" (1966) or Jefferson Airplane's "Crown of Creation" (1968).[52] Some groups used chromatic passing chords to make the harmony seem to slide. In their hit "Incense and Peppermints" (1967), for example, the Strawberry Alarm Clock dynamizes the harmony of the standard "Gloria" progression of garage rock (I-♭VII-IV-I). After converting the progression to dorian (by making the tonic minor), they insert between tonic and subtonic a minor chord built on the leading tone: [i-vii | ♭VII-IV]. Many other chromatic sliding effects appear in the music of Pink Floyd. For instance, in "Astronomy Domine" (1967) the verse begins with a very strong I to VII (not ♭VII) motion; the harmonic transition between verses consists entirely of major triads sliding in half steps from IV down to ♭VII.

Psychedelic groups also exploited the guitar's tone-bending potential, realizing that, as Sam Andrew (Big Brother and the Holding Company) said, "unlike a piano, the guitar had all these microtones, and it was definitely made for psychedelic music."[53] But instead of merely bending the strings with the left hand, they frequently made the guitar pitches slide with a vibrato arm (or "whammy bar")—an arm that, attached to the guitar's bridge, allowed the player to tighten and relax the tension of the strings with the right hand. Introduced on banjos in 1929, vibrato arms had first appeared on electric guitars in the 1940s. During the 1950s some electric guitarists used them to imitate the glissandi of slide trombones (Chet Atkins) or bottleneck guitars (Ike Turner).[54] The most important proto-psychedelic use of vibrato arms, however, was in the surf music of instrumental groups like the Ventures. These groups routinely used vibrato arms to make lower-neighbor embellishing tones or to slide whole chords down and back a half-step.[55] In the aesthetic of surf music, the small glissandi evoked the sound of the Hawaiian guitar and also suggested the undulation of ocean waves. Psychedelic musicians realized that the same technique could suggest the "mind-bending" experience of LSD.

More than other guitarists of his time, Jimi Hendrix fully exploited the vibrato arm. As a left-handed guitarist he played his right-handed Fender Stratocaster "upside-down," which left the vibrato arm *above* the strings (normally it was below). This configuration allowed him to press down the vibrato arm with his forearm while he was playing. Moreover, he had his vibrato arms altered so that he could play glissandi as large as three whole steps in either direction.[56] Such large glissandi, sometimes spread across a full measure or more, transformed the whole structure of guitar harmony. Hendrix used the vibrato arm to turn single notes or chords into chains of glissandi whose speed and width varied continually. The effect became not so much a changing harmony as the dynamic refraction of a single note or chord through a fluid lens.

Some psychedelic players intuitively dynamized harmony with dysfunctional root motion. Sam Andrew explains: "We were able to [go] from C to F♯ without worrying about any kind of transition chord. We could play it first with the animal mind, and then later analyze it." More often, groups used chromatic mediants to dynamize harmony, making the tonality either seem to float or to gravitate to two different tonal centers. Chromatic mediants had appeared in garage rock—I-♭III, for example— and in the music of the Beatles, who often followed a V/V chord with a IV. But psychedelic musicians removed the chords from their diatonic or pentatonic base. One group especially fond of chromatic mediants was the Doors, who were apparently influenced by the chromatic mediants in the opening of "Neptune" in Holst's *The Planets*.[57] The verse of their hit "Light My Fire" consists only of an oscillation between A minor and F♯ minor chords, seeming to hover somewhere slightly removed from the song's principal key (D, as clarified by the chorus). Consider also Iron Butterfly's "In-A-Gadda-Da-Vida" (1968). The song, in D minor, contains a bridge replete with strong non-functional chromatic mediants: alternating G major and E major chords, then A and F♯ major chords, and finally a double chromatic mediant—an emphatic B major chord moving directly to a D minor chord.

Larger-scale chromatic mediant relationships could create a sense of two tonal centers, a "double-tonic complex" (to borrow Robert Bailey's phrase relating to certain late romantic works).[58] Jefferson Airplane's "White Rabbit" divides its polarities between two keys—A major (in the chorus and bridge) and F♯ major (in the verses). These two keys are deployed in a pseudo-flamenco manner: "White Rabbit" dwells extensively on an F♯ major chord, embellished by an upper neighbor chord (G major), which eventually passes up to an A major chord that is then tonicized.[59] The motion from the bridge to the final verse strongly reinforces the song's sense of dual tonality: the bridge, completely diatonic to A major, ends with an A chord, jarringly followed by six measures of an F♯ major chord.

The Doors' "Strange Days" contains an even more overt double-tonic complex, split rather evenly between E and G. The first half of each verse uses only i and iv of E minor; the second half uses i and iv of G minor. (An F♯ major chord separates the two halves.) The chorus consists of the progression G-B-B♭-F-E (all major chords)—which seem to function, respectively, as the tonic of G major, the dominant of E major, the mediant (i.e., relative major chord) of G minor, and the Neapolitan and then tonic of E major. The instrumental break that divides choruses from verses reprises this progression (G-B-B♭-F, three times), then returns to E minor for the beginning of the next verse.

LSD also fostered polytonality. As Paul Kantner explained, playing music while on LSD is "not really conducive to acting functionally together with other people in the right key . . . because people just wander off in other keys."[60] But a few groups purposely simulated that kind of harmonic independence. As early as 1965 the Terrazzo Brothers (later the Mystery Trend) played a polytonal song called "Casbah." The keyboardist recalls that "the lead guitarist put the guitar one fret off, so he'd be playing in one key and I couldn't transpose, so I'm playing in another key and the other guitar player is playing in his own key. So the song was actually being played in three different keys. Complete cacaphonic bedlam and [the audience] loved it!"[61] In its recording "Illusions of My Childhood—Part Two" (1967) Vanilla Fudge plays "Ring Around the Rosies" in three different keys simultaneously. Not all polytonality was quite so blatant. The Bees recorded a psychedelic twelve-bar blues, playfully called "Trip to New Orleans" (1966). Throughout the verse all of the group simultaneously alternates major and minor versions of the same triads each measure. But in the instrumental break the harmonica player continues in the original key of D, while the rest of the ensemble plays a whole step lower.[62]

All of these examples flow from a general "wrong note" aesthetic of psychedelia. As Hendrix ingenuously describes it, psychedelic (or "freak out") technique consists of "playing the opposite notes to what you think the notes should be. . . . It's like playing wrong notes seriously, dig?"[63] One can hear that exemplified in the work of one of Hendrix's psychedelic mentors, Arthur Lee. After hearing Bacharach's "My Little Red Book" in the Woody Allen movie *What's New Pussycat?* (1966), Lee arranged it in "wrong-note" style. He completely shifts the relation of melody to chords in the song's opening, adds chromatic neighbor chords, and occasionally divides the melody and harmony so as to create disturbing half-step clashes, as if the voice and accompaniment had veered into separate keys. (A similar half-step clash appears in the Doors' "Light My Fire," about which more later.)

*

In 1966 Timothy Leary proposed a plan for a "hallucinatory art." The first step, he said, was for the artist to take a hallucinogenic drug that would lead him "into a kaleidoscopic flow of direct energy—swirling patterns of capillary coiling." Second, "in order to communicate his hallucination" the artist needed to have "access to energy-transforming machines which duplicate the capillary flow."[64] Psychedelic rock became the perfect vehicle for this kind of art. Rock musicians could take "energy transforming" devices from the past and present of popular music, try to "duplicate the capillary flow," and effectively liquify many sonic parameters.

Guitarists used the "wah-wah" pedal to dynamize the tone of the instrument. As early as the 1920s jazz trumpeters had embellished their solos with the "wah-wah" effect of fanning the cup of a sink plunger in front of the instrument's bell. Chet Atkins adapted the effect for guitar in his "Boo Boo Stick Beat" (1959), playing chordal riffs through a volume pedal whose volume circuit he replaced with a tone control circuit.[65] In the mid-1960s some companies introduced pre-made "wah-wah" pedals. Popularized by Eric Clapton (in Cream's "Tales of Brave Ulysses," 1967, and "White Room," 1968) and by Hendrix (the *Electric Ladyland* album, 1968), the wah-wah pedal became a psychedelic mannerism—something that made guitar tone sound, in Hendrix's words, "like something is reaching out."[66]

Rock singers dynamized their voices in various ways. Using vocal techniques borrowed from jazz, Grace Slick often modulated from one vowel sound to another or merged vowels with consonants—as in the word "be" in the first line of "Somebody to Love" (1967), which she sings across a glissando and gradually melds into the "L" of the following word, "lies."

Engineer Al Schmitt reports that she also tried other, more exotic means to dynamize the sound of her voice: "She would turn her head from left to right to create weird but interesting nasal noises. On other days she would keep changing her position from left to right in front of the microphone to see what changes she could create in her own tonalities."[67] Most singers, however, used electronic manipulation to dynamize their voices. John Lennon sent the amplified sound of his voice through a revolving Leslie organ speaker in "Tomorrow Never Knows" (1966)—creating a dynamic whooshing sound that was copied in subsequent recordings by the Beatles, Family, the Grateful Dead, and others.[68] Some added echo effects to do electronically what Sean Bonniwell and others had done physically, dynamizing the words at phrase endings: "play-yay-yay-yay," for example, in the Lemon Pipers' "Green Tambourine" (1967), or "sou-wow-wow-wow-nd" in Big Brother and the Holding Company's "Light Is Faster Than Sound" (1967).

Guitarists used feedback to dynamize both tone and pitch. In the opening to "I Feel Fine" (1964), the Beatles had converted feedback from a transient flaw of amplified music into a timbre modulating device: McCartney plucks the A string of his bass and Lennon deliberately allows sympathetic feedback from his guitar.[69] Hendrix uses feedback similarly for the opening of "Foxy Lady" (1967), only louder and longer, turning feedback into a kind of psychedelic fanfare. Such feedback fanfaring also appears at the beginning of songs by Jefferson Airplane and Steppenwolf.[70] Some guitarists dynamized their solos by holding a climactic pitch with their left hand and using feedback to simmer it from one timbre or overtone to another. Hendrix further embellished this kind of feedback. He would strike a single string, approach the amplifier, and swing his guitar in front of it (to vary the feedback) while bending the string with his right hand and playing the vibrato arm with his left.[71]

In 1966 the Beatles' producer George Martin reversed the direction of the vocal track tape for the last verse of the song "Rain."[72] Other groups soon followed his example, backtracking one or more tracks of their recordings. Backtracking conveys a "psychedelic" sound because it changes the decays of notes into attacks, an effect resembling what one LSD user described: the drug made things seem "as if the essence of the underlying idea were struggling or pressing, rather, to reveal itself."[73] The new attacks of backtracked music seemed more like coagulations, still "molten" and "dripping," to borrow Leary's words. Guitarists could dynamize their articulation with backtracking just as they had dynamized their tone with feedback (see especially Hendrix's "Are You Experienced?" 1967). And Moby Grape and the First Edition used solo backtracked guitars as other groups had used feedback—for psychedelic fanfaring at the beginning of songs.[74]

In 1959 recording engineer Larry Levine inadvertently discovered a sound effect that would become a psychedelic cliché. By superimposing two identical dubs of the same material played at minutely different speeds, he got a composite sound that seemed to "whoosh" like the air plowing of a jet airplane. (This sound dominates the resulting Toni Fisher recording, "The Big Hurt.")[75] Beginning in 1965, the Beatles used a variant of this technique to give a choric effect to their vocal tracks; the technical name their engineers gave it was "automatic double tracking" or "ADT."[76] In "Blue Jay Way" (1967), George Harrison took the ADT so far out of phase as to surpass the eerie effect of "The Big Hurt."[77] Other rock musicians began using the same effect, which became known as "phasing." Some of the occurrences of phasing were inadvertent—as was the case with Count Five's "Psychotic Reaction."[78] Some groups used phasing to make a general hallucinatory impression, as in the Small Faces' "Itchycoo Park" (1967, on the words "I feel inclined to blow my mind" and "It's all too beautiful"). Eric Burdon and the Animals, however, used phasing to text-paint the very specific image of a jet plane in "Sky Pilot" (1968). Hendrix used phasing extensively, saying that it resembled the "underwater sound" he had heard in his "dreams," presumably including LSD visions. His producer recalls: "I had been experimenting with phasing and its possible uses for Hendrix, and when I played the results for him he yelled, 'That's it! That's the sound . . . in my dreams.'"[79] Hendrix later described phasing thus: "It makes a sound like planes going through your membranes and chromosomes."[80]

Finally, some groups dynamized their recordings spatially by using stereo panning to make the sound glide between left and right speakers. Early stereo records of the 1950s had tried to recreate the "living sound" of the concert hall, with instruments positioned across a three-dimensional aural field. In the late 1950s several percussion ensemble records featured responsories between instruments separated into their respective stereo channels. (This was called "ping-pong sound.")[81] In the early 1960s a few bands finally used stereo panning as a novelty, an effect called by one label "the exciting new illusion of sound in motion."[82] Against the background of these recordings—and with the stimulus of Stockhausen's electronic compositions—psychedelic musicians often panned their music across stereo channels. Records by the Grateful Dead, Jefferson Airplane, the Mothers, and Hendrix all abound with the technique, sometimes in free-form "collage" pieces.

Feedback and phasing had been flaws of the past; wah-wah, backtracking, and stereo panning had been novelties. But all of them became fundamentals of "hallucinatory" art in music. Psychedelic groups consistently pushed their music through a host of "energy transforming machines" that began with no drug connotations but came to acquire them. One LSD user remarked that the drug made phenomena seem as if they were "programmed to go through synapses that make patterns on everything."[83] In dynamizing their raw sonorities psychedelic groups symbolically sent their music through electronic synapses that made patterns everywhere.

*

Here then is how one might best use the word "psychedelic" to describe a rock style. "Psychedelic" is extremely loud, reverberant, contrapuntal rock, slowed in tempo, unstable in harmony, and juxtapositional in form. What is more, to be truly "psychedelic" at least some of the music's parameters must go through devices that create "molten" shapes in timbre, articulation, and spatial placement. Psychedelic music dechronicizes and depersonalizes the listener through its excessive length, repetition, volume, and spatial depth. It then dynamizes the familiar forms, harmonies, and sonic details of rock through methods indebted to surf music, free jazz, musique concrète, and assorted technologies. In these ways, the freewheeling multi-leveled ornamentations of psychedelic music enable rock to explore its most primal impulse: to become like the world Albert Hofmann discovered, inhabited by objects that are "in constant motion, animated, as if driven by an inner restlessness."

And in that respect, psychedelic music parallels the activism of the garage bands. Garage rock celebrated activism through sheer speed and a sense of restlessness—but always confined within narrow limits. Garage rock was largely a matter of musical treadmilling. But the restlessness of psychedelic music was that of a quasi-Baroque embellishment of every parameter.

Psychedelic rock also provided a counterpart to the antagonism of garage rock. Garage rock showed contempt for the trappings of middle- and upper-class society, partly through music that defied conventional notions of pure tone, proper diction, and strong harmonic progressions. Psychedelic rock was more subversive, using new forms, unusual chord progressions, sophisticated technology, and novel gadgets to undermine the conventions of popular music and, implicitly, of the whole cultural environment. Psychedelic musicians even attacked the short-lived conventions of rock music, dynamizing them for all subsequent generations of rock musicians.[84]

An early promotional photo for the best known of the Pacific Northwest garage bands, Paul Revere and the Raiders, whose hits featured the "post-Holly" vocal techniques of Mark Lindsay (far left). (Neal Skok Archives)

HUNGRY

Words and Music by BARRY MANN and CYNTHIA WEIL

Recorded by
PAUL REVERE
and THE RAIDERS
on COLUMBIA RECORDS

KEYS
04706
SCREEN GEMS-COLUMBIA MUSIC , INC.
75¢

The title page of the Raiders' hit "Hungry," which incorporated such garage rock traits as the "rhythmic monad" and the "Empty Heart" harmonic progression. (Neal Skok Archives)

Opposite page: The Seeds, whose music exemplified garage rock in its two-chord oscillations and the "post-Jagger/post-Holly" vocals of lead singer Sky Saxon (second from left). As in this promotional photo, middle-class suburban garage bands often aspired to an image that was lower-class and urban. (Neal Skok Archives)

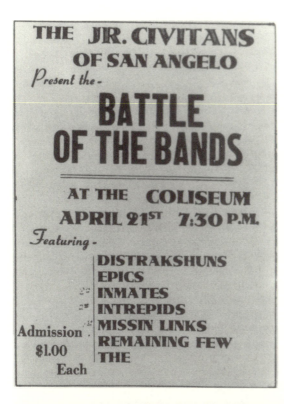

THE JR. CIVITANS
OF SAN ANGELO
Present the -

BATTLE
OF THE BANDS

AT THE   COLISEUM
APRIL 21ST 7:30 P.M.

Featuring -

DISTRAKSHUNS
EPICS
INMATES
INTREPIDS
MISSIN LINKS
REMAINING FEW
THE

Admission .
$1.00
Each

Many garage bands got record contracts by winning a "battle of the bands," such as the one advertised here. The group names in this 1967 contest suggest how sixties groups often defined themselves: as alienated, primitive, or even criminal—and sometimes misspelled their names to create word plays (e.g., the Dis-trak*shuns*). (Michael Hicks Archives)

This handbill from the Fort Worth Teen Fair and Mardi Gras Festival shows how garage bands like the Seeds and the McCoys, psychedelic bands like the Doors and the Electric Prunes, and "mainstream" artists like Every Mother's Son and Sonny and Cher collectively represented "pop music" in 1967. (Greg Shaw Archives)

An Invitation To Blow Your Mind!
POP MUSIC FESTIVAL
Will Rogers ExhiLit Bldg.
Ft. Worth 30 Mins. Down Turnpike
August 26th Thru September 4th
(Labor Day)
THE DOORS "Light My Fire"
THE BOX TOPS "The Letter"
THE STANDELLS "Dirty Water"
THE SEEDS "Can't Seem to Make You Mine"
THE GRASS ROOTS "Live For Today"
EVERY MOTHERS' SON
"Down to My Boat"
THE McCOYS "Hang on Sloopy"
THE ELECTRIC PRUNES
"I Had Too Much to Dream"
*SONNY & CHER "Need We List?"
Admission—$2.00
*TENTATIVE

Joined by KJR program director Pat O'Day (third from right), the Kingsmen, best known for their version of "Louie Louie" (1963), hold a Jolly Green Giant doll in celebration of their hit of the same name (1965). (Neal Skok Archives)

Billy Roberts, writer of "Hey Joe," in a promotional photo from the early 1960s. (June Johnson and William Moses Roberts Jr.)

Los Angeles–based garage band the Standells, one of the dozens of groups to record "Hey Joe" in the 1960s. (Promotional photo in Neal Skok Archives)

One of the finest "post-Jagger" vocalists, Sean Bonniwell fronted the Music Machine, a group whose slow, introspective version of "Hey Joe" influenced other artists to rewrite the song. (Promotional photo in Neal Skok Archives)

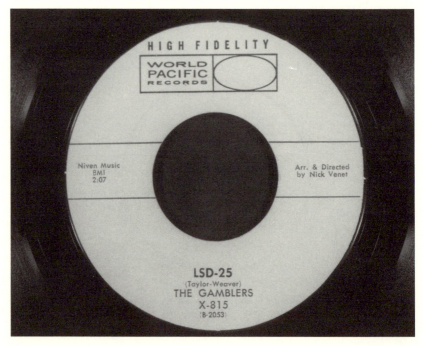

This simple surf instrumental was (almost inadvertently) the first record to refer to LSD. (Michael Hicks Archives)

The Surfaris (probably the first group to record "Hey Joe") typified surf groups who used the Fender Stratocaster vibrato arm (far left) for tone-bending—a practice later identified with the dynamization of pitch in psychedelic music. (Promotional photo in Robert Dalley Archives)

Iron Butterfly, whose "In-A-Gadda-Da-Vida" (1968) typified psychedelic music's slower tempos, nonfunctional harmonic progressions, wah-wah guitar, deep reverberation, and extreme length. (Promotional photo in Michael Hicks Archives)

A Vancouver handbill for one of the many events inspired by Ken Kesey's Trips Festival and Acid Tests (1965–66)—events that were the cradles of psychedelic music and multimedia rock concerts. (Neal Skok Archives)

Captain Consciousness presents.....a Centennial Event

THE TRIP: AN ELECTRONIC PERFORMANCE

vancouver's first festival of sound & light
an ecstatic new space total sense perception

Friday the grateful dead — the acid test — weco multi-visual projection — the pH factor jug band — super-stroboscopic lighting gerry walker tape music — the daily flash —— the DANCE

Saturday big brother & the holding company — gary lee nova's magic mirrors liquid injection—projection — the daily flash — electronic music al neil & his royal canadians — jesse — the pH factor — the grateful dead & the unexpectable

Sunday al neil jazz trio (royal rascals)
movies: Charlie Chaplin: the vagabond — the gambler; Andy Warhol: Harlot; Harry Smith shorts! new film by sam perry - shorts by gary lee nova
michael mcClure does his thing bill bissett the pH factor — big brother & the holding co. the grateful dead — the daily flash & DANCE

18 & over only   Is this your place in the rock revolution keep listening to C-Fun for more details

doors open at p.n.e. garden auditorium
8:30 p.m.
. advance tickets $2.00 per nite $5.00 for series

The Blind Owl · The Pot Shoppe · Positively Fourth Street
2057 w. 4th   1420 w. pender 2137 w. fourth
736-6177

Record Gallery
936 Robson st.

| black lite provided wear your best fluorescent clothes & makeup |

McLeods Books
350 w. pender

Tickets at the door

$2.50 per nite $6.00 for series

A handbill for a 1966 event featuring the 13th Floor Elevators, the first rock group to use the word "psychedelic" in an album title. (Neal Skok Archives)

Opposite page: This handbill from Bill Graham's Fillmore Auditorium concert series—a series inspired by Kesey's Trips Festival—pairs two artists closely associated with "Hey Joe": Jimi Hendrix, who recorded it as his first single, and Dino Valenti, who initially claimed to have written the song. The psychedelic artwork is by Rick Griffin, who earlier had gained fame as the chief cartoonist for *Surfer* magazine. (Michael Hicks Archives)

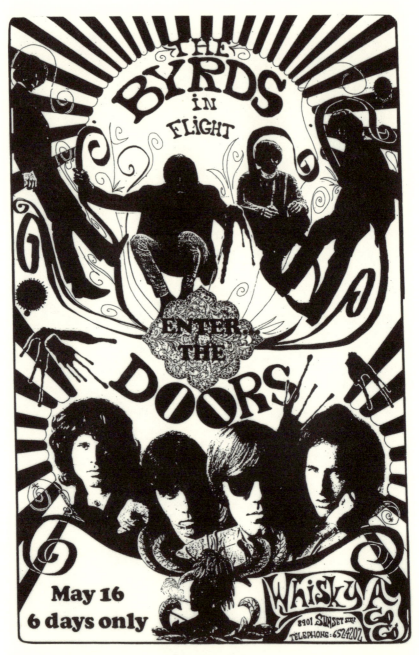

This 1967 engagement united two groups, both of whom had previously been house bands at the Whisky A Go Go: the Byrds, the already legendary band who popularized "Hey Joe" in Los Angeles, and the Doors, whose single "Light My Fire" was about to enter the charts, eventually becoming the Number 1 song in the country. (Greg Shaw Archives)

A 1967 advertisement for the shortened version of "Light My Fire," which was already, as the ad says, "blazing beyond control" and "consuming the country." (Greg Shaw Archives)

The psychedelic practice of experimenting with the endings of recordings can be traced back to this 1946 record—the first to actually *end* a song with a fade. (Michael Hicks Archives)

A detail from *Da Capo* (1967), the second album by Love—yet another group that recorded "Hey Joe," and one who, on this album, recorded perhaps the first substitution ending (in the song "Seven and Seven Is"). (Michael Hicks Archives)

6 Playing with "Fire"

The Doors took their name from Aldous Huxley's *The Doors of Perception,*
a seminal book on hallucinogenic drugs. Not surprisingly, much of the
Doors' music meets our criteria for "psychedelic": songs are long, jazz-
influenced, unusual in formal design, filled with chromatic mediants, and
heavy with reverberation. The best example is their first hit record, "Light
My Fire." Released in April 1967, it entered the Top 100 on June 3 and eventually spent nine weeks in the Top 10—three of them as the Number-1
record in the country. The song dominated the American airwaves during the summer of 1967 and seemed to connect with many of the societal
upheavals of the moment. Although essentially a love song, "Light My
Fire" acquired other connotations: its imagery made it a veritable theme
song for arsonists in racial uprisings, for soldiers in Vietnam, and for people who smoked pot.[1] For these reasons, the song has been called "the
anthem of a generation," not to mention one of "the best singles ever
made."[2]

The way the Doors composed "Light My Fire" shows how diverse
musical sources could converge into a "psychedelic" whole. The way mass
culture coopted "Light My Fire" shows how a strikingly unusual rock song
could quickly become a pop standard. And the Doors' persistent muta-
tions of the song in performance suggest how a late-1960s rock group
could continue embellishing a work on stage, long after it was "finished"
in the recording studio.[3] In what follows we will see how the Doors first

assembled the song, then continually reworked it, as if to keep reclaiming it as their own at a time when it was becoming an international pop phenomenon.

*

At an early rehearsal in December 1965, singer Jim Morrison asked the other members of the group to write some songs. Guitarist Robby Krieger recalls that, in order to compete with Morrison's mystical texts, he would try to write lyrics around the four elements—earth, air, fire, water. Krieger returned the next day with two new songs, both composed in about an hour. For one of them he chose the image of fire, partly because he liked the Rolling Stones' song "Play With Fire."[4]

When he presented the song to the group, the lyrics consisted of two verses and a chorus.[5] The verse melody resembled perhaps a Beatles melody, only more single-minded in its redundancy (Ex. 7a).[6] The chords beneath the melody alternated between A and F♯ minor—although, as Krieger then played it, the A chord was not clearly minor or major, since he omitted the third.[7] The chorus melody consisted of the roots of its accompanying chords—G, A, D, and E (Ex. 8a). When Krieger played through the song, organist Ray Manzarek considered "Light My Fire" a "vaguely Sonny and Cher, sort of Mamas and Papas sounding . . . . jug band kind of song."[8] Densmore recalled that it "immediately sounded like a hit single to me. It had a hook. It stuck in your memory the moment you heard it."[9]

Densmore and Manzarek began to revise "Light My Fire." Densmore altered the rhythmic character of the verses by superimposing a simplified rumba drum pattern, reverting to the standard rock backbeat only in the chorus. Meanwhile, Manzarek interpreted Krieger's A chord as A *minor*.[10] And he asked the other players to leave the room while he wrote an introduction. During this time, he recalls, "all my Bach training came back"; he tried to build his introduction from the circle-of-fifths chord progression he had learned in music theory training. But what he produced—a florid, pseudo-Baroque melody above a four-measure progression of major triads and major-minor seventh chords (G-D7 | F-B♭7 | E♭-A♭ | A)—was not quite what he originally intended: the first fifth ascends, followed by an ascending minor third, three descending fifths, and an ascending minor second.[11] Since the song still lacked a bridge, Manzarek suggested a solo section in the middle: "I said to John, 'Let's do like Elvin Jones and John Coltrane, "My Favorite Things."' So I soloed and then Robby soloed and we came back to the song, two more choruses and out."[12]

Example 7. "Light My Fire" First-Verse Melody. In the original version, the A minor chord has no third; hence, both C and C♯ are possible.

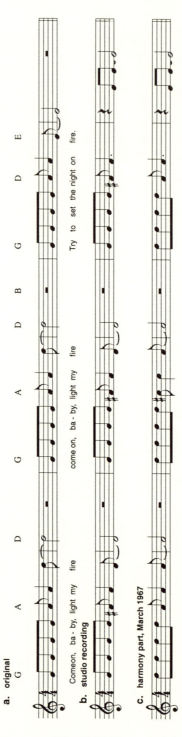

a. original

Comeon, ba - by, light my fire   come on, ba - by, light my fire   Try to set the night on fire.

b. studio recording

c. harmony part, March 1967

Example 8. "Light My Fire" Chorus

Morrison also began revising, though by all accounts unwittingly. He tried singing Krieger's melody, but Manzarek's decision about the A chord made the melody less singable than when Krieger had presented it. Besides, the inexperienced Morrison may have had a poor memory for melody. He spontaneously "created his own [verse] melody from within [Krieger's]" and Krieger accepted it.[13] Morrison also changed the shape of the chorus, descending instead of ascending on the words "light my," and thereby creating an added-sixth chord on the dominant (Ex. 8b).

When the Doors recorded their first album in September 1966, they made a long, energetic take of "Light My Fire" the closing song of the first side. For some reason, however, the producers slowed the recording down slightly, lowering the key almost a half step and deepening Morrison's voice. This slowing exacerbated some confusion about the song's duration. The record label and record jacket printed the duration as 6:30 and 6:50, respectively; the actual playing time was 7:05. The real length of this take of "Light My Fire," however—based on speeding up the record slightly to regain the original pitch level—is approximately 6:45.

As a diagram of the recording suggests, the length, formal design, harmonic structure, and stylistic diversity bespoke psychedelic eclecticism and dynamization (Figure 1). On the surface, the music reflected diverse influences: Baroque keyboard music in the A section, Latin dance music

A instrumental passage (five measures [IV-V7/IV | $^\flat$III-V7/II$^\flat$ | $^\flat$II-$^\flat$V | V | V])

B verse 1 (eight measures: alternating A minor and F♯ minor chords, one measure each—[v | iii])

C chorus (six measures: [IV-V | I | IV-V | V-V/ii | IV-I | V/V])

B^1 verse 2

C

D "solo section" (featuring organ and guitar solos over one-measure ostinato bass line outlining contiguous triads [v-vi])

A

B^1 "third" verse (same as verse 2)

C

B^3 "fourth" verse (verse 1 with altered melody)

C^1 chorus text, with altered melody and extension to a total of fourteen measures: the line "try to set the night on fire" is sung four times over a new, two-measure chord progression ($^\flat$III-$^\flat$VII | I)

A

Figure 1. The Plan of "Light My Fire." Roman numerals refer to the main key of the song (D), as defined by the chorus.

in the B section, standard rock in the C section, and modal jazz in the D section. At a deeper level, the music explored several harmonic regions. The opening chords of the A section (G-D7) suggested I and V^7 of G major; the progression in the C section clearly denoted D major; the D section suggested A dorian; while the B section's alternating A minor and F♯ minor chords left the tonality ambivalent.

We should examine the verse melody (B section) and the solo section (D) fairly closely, since in performance the Doors altered these two sections most. The verse melody is a small X-X-X'-X structure based on a simple oscillation between C and A, the respective thirds of the A minor and F♯ minor chords. These notes provided a framework for Morrison, who added passing tones and an unaccented appoggiatura (Ex. 7b). In the *last* verse, however, Morrison sang a permutated transposition of the X' idea, changing what was an unaccented appoggiatura into an accented incomplete neighbor. This alteration creates a strong sense of drama, as the strong D at the end of each line clashes with the C♯ of the accompanying F♯ minor chord (Ex. 9a).

The solo section is a gloss on Coltrane's "My Favorite Things." The solos in both "Light My Fire" and "My Favorite Things" rely on hypnotic harmony, with dorian melodies above an oscillation of two minor triads a major second apart (in the Doors' case A minor and B minor; in Coltrane's, E minor and F♯ minor). In both cases, the absence of harmonic "progression" demands that the solo melodies project clear architectures of their own. In both songs, the static bass line also impels the drummer to provide responsorial material throughout. As Densmore puts it, "there wasn't a big bass filling the sound, so I was free to mess around."[14]

The solo section of the studio recording of "Light My Fire" consists of four subsections—the organ solo, the guitar solo, the contrapuntal duo, and the retransition—each of them shorter than the previous (Fig. 2a). The organ and guitar solos both use a chain-link pattern, in which a motive appears then immediately repeats with some variation or extension that generates a new motive. To create momentum, Manzarek combines this design with several techniques: shortening the length of motives to be repeated;[15] reducing the average note value; thickening the texture (to four-voice chords at the climax); raising the tessitura; and introducing syncopations and supertriplets. Similarly, Krieger creates momentum by gradually lifting the tessitura and shortening note values. But his solo, unlike Manzarek's, proceeds in fits and starts. He reveals his flamenco roots via rhetorical pauses, terse statements of rapid-note figures, and modal shifts from dorian to aeolian.[16]

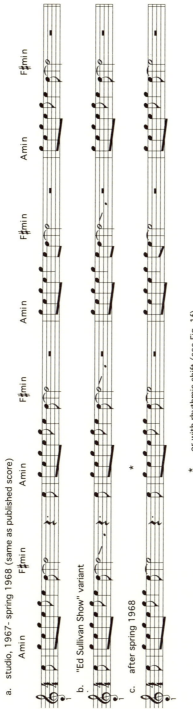

a. studio, 1967– spring 1968 (same as published score)

b. "Ed Sullivan Show" variant

c. after spring 1968

*

* or with rhythmic shift (see Fig. 1f)

Example 9. "Light My Fire" Last-Verse Melody

a. studio (September 1966)

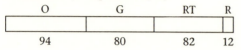

b. Stockholm (20 September 1968)

c. Vancouver (June 1970)

Figure 2. "Light My Fire" Solo Section. Shown are the relative proportions of the organ solo (O), guitar solo (G), contrapuntal duo (CD), responsorial trio (RT), quotation of standards (QS), and retransition (R). The number of measures appears below each subsection. In each case the first subsection (O) includes all material from the end of the second chorus to the beginning of the guitar solo. In parts b and c the third subsection (RT or QS) includes the solo bass ostinato that precedes the retransition.

The contrapuntal duo begins when Krieger reprises his opening motive (4:43 on the recording), which Manzarek imitates. The two then interweave improvised lines until the beginning of the retransition, where Krieger introduces a repeated-note figure on a supertriplet + half-note (5:13). As Krieger continues playing that figure, both Densmore and Manzarek join in playing likewise. Six measures after the initial statement of the figure, all of the players begin playing continuous supertriplets in independent conjunct lines of pitch. This retransition leads back to a reprise of the organ introduction (A section).[17]

*

By the spring of 1967, a few FM stations were playing the studio recording of "Light My Fire." But AM stations refused to play it because it was too long. According to Densmore, disc jockey Dave Diamond persuaded him and Robby that a shortened version could be a hit.[18] So producer Paul Rothchild prepared an edited version that omits the entire solo section—except for the retransition, the beginning of which provided a perfect place to splice the tape. Manzarek felt that the edit gutted the recording, because he considered the solo section not only "the heart and the soul" of "Light My Fire," but "virtually the whole point of the song."[19] Nevertheless, he conceded that the short version (a mere 2:52) had commercial potential.[20] As it turned out, once the single became popular, the same radio stations that rejected the long version now *chose* to play the original album version. To do so not only showed that a disc jockey was "hip," but, as Geoffrey Stokes remarks, it was "entirely consistent with the tight playlist philosophy—why have a hit hold your listeners for three minutes when it can hold them for seven?"[21]

The Doors performed the edited version only on television. On American Bandstand and similar shows they simply lip-synched the single. On the Jonathan Winters Show they closely replicated the single, except in the last chorus, where Morrison's voice gave out. (The performance was also marred by Morrison's leap into a rope fence on the stage, which he knocked down and tangled around him.)[22] The best-known and musically most interesting television performance of "Light My Fire" was on the Ed Sullivan Show in September 1967. The story of the producer's attempts to persuade Morrison to change the lyrics is well-known. (The sponsors required that he scrap the line "girl, we couldn't get much higher," but he sang it anyway, blacklisting the group from any further appearances.) But more significant is how the group tried to edit the song in a way different from Rothchild. At the end of the second chorus, Manzarek vamps for only two measures (instead of the four on the record), then solos for three measures—a fast, highly ornamented allusion to the studio version. The group then plays the retransition, but for only four measures. These changes produce a more balanced reduction of the original studio version than did the simple splice. The performance is significant in another way. Morrison begins each line of the last verse as in the studio recording, but slides down a perfect fourth to the third of the F♯ minor triad (Ex. 9b). This is the earliest recorded hint that Morrison was troubled by the dissonance of the studio version. In time, Morrison would evade the dissonance altogether.

*

The earliest extant live recording of "Light My Fire," 10 March 1967, shows that the Doors were still experimenting with the song's elements after making the studio recording. In this performance they remove the organ introduction in favor of a gradual layering of parts: Krieger plays the verse chords solo for four measures; Densmore and Manzarek join in for four more measures, after which Morrison enters. What had been the organ introduction then becomes a *bridge* between the first chorus and second verse.[23] Moreover, Manzarek adds a vocal harmony to the chorus (Ex. 8c). The Doors may have realized that none of these modifications could improve on the studio version, since no subsequent live recordings contain them.

Beginning in summer 1967, the Doors refined and stylized the song in the hundreds of live concerts that followed the success of the single version of "Light My Fire." They also tried to play "Light My Fire" at a strategic place in their program, directly following portions of their avant-garde theater piece, "The Celebration of the Lizard." Immediately at the end of the aleatory, pointillistic music of "Celebration," Densmore played the snare drum crack that announced "Light My Fire," leaving no break between the two. This elision had a twofold effect. From an aesthetic perspective it was just the sort of juxtaposition of opposites that the Doors—especially Morrison—savored. But from a practical perspective, going directly from "Celebration" into "Light My Fire" allayed the awkward response that the former was sure to receive from its listeners. If "Celebration" could expect bewildered silence, "Light My Fire" would provoke cheers.[24]

In this period the organ and guitar solos evolved differently. While Manzarek continued to shape his solo according to a basic rise and fall of intensity, he seldom limited himself to the specific musical ideas of the studio version. He reinvented his solo at each concert, beginning it in one of four ways: (1) as in the studio version, (2) with a compound melody featuring recurring drone notes, (3) with a fast, florid riff that hinted of Krieger's flamenco style, or (4) with a series of terse, staccato utterances that gradually accelerated and coalesced. Depending less and less on the supertriplets that characterized his studio solo, he increased the overall rhythmic interest, often by using rapidly repeated notes in fast subdivisions of the beat. He also continued to use the dorian mode almost exclusively, except at the climax, which he sometimes tried to intensify by adding thick tone clusters. By mid-1968 he often followed the climax of his solo with a long, delicate passage, sometimes using the accelerando idea mentioned above and a different organ stop. This practice tended to divide his solo into two distinct, contrasting parts.

Meanwhile, all of Krieger's recorded solos from this period derived overtly from the studio solo. He began every one identically, and the successive motifs of the studio version appeared as clear signposts throughout the course of the solo. Between them, he either developed the ideas differently from the studio version or played contrasting ideas, often blues-derived. He continued to alternate dorian and aeolian modes, but added more tone bending and occasionally disoriented the listener's sense of tonality with a chain of chromatically sliding dyads. Sometime around the fall of 1968, Krieger began to introduce quotations from the verse, bridge, and chorus of the Beatles' "Eleanor Rigby," whose conjunct dorian lines dovetailed with his own.

During this period the Doors also revamped the sixteen-measure contrapuntal duo. While they sometimes played the duo as in the studio recording, they often replaced it (or followed it) with a series of responsories. After the guitar solo Krieger and/or Manzarek improvised terse, percussive figures—sometimes with organ clusters or damped guitar strings, and sometimes a quote from "Eleanor Rigby"—which, in turn, Densmore and/or Manzarek echoed. (For a sample of the responsorial technique, see Ex. 10).[25] Gradually, they dissipated the responsorial ideas until only Manzarek's keyboard bass remained. Manzarek continued his bass ostinato indefinitely until Morrison cued the retransition. Densmore explained that, at this point in the song, Morrison "would purposely wait until everyone, especially me, got very restless"—leaving the keyboard bass playing solo for as long as twenty measures.[26]

When Morrison did cue them, the players began the supertriplet-plus-half-note-retransition motive *subito fortissimo e marcato.* They also expanded the retransition from the original ten measures to sixteen or more, obviously trying to heighten the drama of the passage. But they seem to have realized that the extension didn't work. Not only was the rhythmic idea too simple to warrant so many repetitions, but for some reason the players almost invariably dragged the tempo of the supertriplets, creating a sense of inertia instead of momentum. By the fall of 1968, the group had learned to stay in tempo and had cut the retransition back to about twelve measures. This became more or less the standard length from then on.[27]

By making the changes discussed here, the Doors more clearly partitioned the solo section into its four subsections: the organ solo, the guitar solo, the contrapuntal duo/responsorial trio, and the retransition. Sometimes they divided these further into (a) two distinct parts to the organ solo, and (b) two distinct parts following the guitar solo—that is, a contrapuntal duo *and* a responsorial trio. Generally, the organ solo, guitar solo, and contrapuntal duo/responsorial trio were near equal in length, although the organ solo was always the longest. The solo section performed during their first show at Stockholm, 20 September 1968, was typical in its proportions as well as its overall length (see Fig. 2b).

Example 10. Responsorial Techniques in Solo Section of "Light My Fire," Stockholm, 20 September 1968

Densmore recalls that the solo section of "Light My Fire" was one of the few continuing pleasures of the group's touring career—"I always looked forward to it," he wrote. "When it was good, you wanted the groove to go on forever."[28] But the song grated on Morrison. Manzarek recalls, "Jim objected to doing 'Light My Fire' [because] he had to do it the same way every night, but we got to stretch out for . . . however long we wanted for our solos."[29] This situation posed an artistic problem for Morrison, who despised conformity and consistency. It also posed a marketing problem for the band, since Morrison had become the sex symbol/star of the group and the main draw for all of their performances. Instead of being a musical high point—a "gorgeous wall of noise," one observer called it[30]—the solo section of "Light My Fire" became the one portion of the concert where Morrison had virtually nothing to do. (One writer said that the solos seemed to function as accompaniments to "Morrison's lapses of interest.")[31] On both accounts, aesthetics and public relations, it was inevitable that Morrison would try to involve himself in the solo section.

Even in the earliest performances of "Light My Fire" Morrison wandered the stage during the solos, engaging in various antics.[32] As the dimensions of the solo section expanded in late 1967–68, Morrison augmented his theatrics, using the solo section to wander offstage, dance, banter with the audience, or get them to clap the backbeat. Sometimes he simply slumped down dramatically in front of the drums, remaining motionless until it was time to cue the retransition. As the band played larger venues, Morrison exaggerated his behavior, explaining that with more space "it's necessary to project more . . . almost to the point of grotesqueness. I think when you're a small dot at the end of a large arena, you have to make up for that lack of intimacy with expanded movement."[33] For that reason, he became somewhat ferocious, ripping off his bead necklace and throwing it, knocking over the mike stand, destroying the microphone itself, or jumping off the stage into the audience, all during or just after the solos. The audience began to respond with its own theatrics: during "Light My Fire" they lit matches and sparklers and threw them onto the stage.[34]

During this period, Morrison brought vocal ideas into the instrumental solo section. Between the organ and guitar solos he approached the microphone and intoned two brief lines from the middle of the song "When the Music's Over": "Persian night, babe / See the light, babe." More strikingly, when the retransition motive began, he held the microphone against his mouth and screamed the word "fuck" repeatedly, in rhythm, for three measures or more (the barking sound that one hears during this passage on most live recordings). This was probably not a spontaneous vulgarism, but rather, a kind of quotation from another Doors song, "The End." Paul Rothchild explains that in the Oedipal section of the studio recording of "The End," Morrison shouted the word "fuck" over and over "as a rhythm instrument, which is what we intended it to be."[35] That "rhythm instrument" was buried in the studio mix of "The End." Now, forcefully superimposed on "Light My Fire," it shocked many a fan who had come to hear the group's most famous song.

Morrison also pared down the verse melody. By the fall of 1967 he had already eliminated the passing tones in the first three verses; all that remained was a series of minor thirds with the unaccented appoggiatura on the third line of each verse (Ex. 7c). Sometime during summer 1968 he eliminated the appoggiatura as well, so that all of the first three verses consisted only of oscillating minor thirds (Ex. 7d). More important, he removed the dramatic dissonant tone at the end of each line of the fourth verse and turned the last verse into a series of minor thirds—simply a dominant-level transposition of the earlier verses (Ex. 9c).[36]

*

In the summer and fall of 1968 two events drastically affected the Doors' relationship to their own song. One was the July release of a pop cover version of the song by Latino singer José Feliciano. His version omits most of the elements of "Light My Fire" that made it psychedelic and adds others that made it pop. Feliciano strips down the form, cutting the introduction and solo section. He removes completely the dissonance that Morrison had used in the last verse of the original hit. He slows the tempo, making the beat resemble a cha-cha, plays a short pseudo-flamenco guitar solo in place of one of the verses, and adds a lush string arrangement. Rather than end decisively, as the Doors' version did, Feliciano's fades out over a vamp on the verse chords.

The success of Feliciano's "Light My Fire" rivaled that of the Doors' original. It spent twelve weeks on the charts, half of those in the Top 10, where it reached Number 3. For his version of the song Feliciano received the Grammy Award for Best Contemporary Male Pop Vocal Performance and was voted Best New Artist of 1968 by the National Academy of Recording Arts and Sciences—the same institution that had completely ignored the Doors the previous year. Feliciano's mainstream acclaim encouraged pop artists of all kinds to cover the song. That acclaim also precipitated the second crucial event in the Doors' relationship to "Light My Fire."

After the group's European tour in fall 1968, the Buick corporation offered to buy the song for a new jingle—"Come on Buick, light my fire." The three instrumentalists agreed to the sale. Manzarek later argued that it was not so much the money that attracted him to the offer as "for rock and roll to actually penetrate the mainstream, that could be one of the most subversive things you could do. Right in . . . *America's* living room, here's psychedelic rock and roll!"[37] But since the song was a collaborative effort, the rights had been assigned to the entire group. Morrison vetoed the agreement, raging over his friends' decision to commercialize the song.[38]

By the year's end, dozens of pop artists had covered "Light My Fire." Torch singers such as Jack Jones, Julie London, and Johnny Mathis sang the song in recorded versions derived from Feliciano's. Orchestras (such as Nelson Riddle's) and small pop ensembles (such as Young-Holt Unlimited) recorded the song in post-Feliciano versions that could best be categorized as "easy listening" or "mood music." The Doors had seen their song become a standard, but one completely disconnected from their own aesthetic. The popularity of the reconstituted "Light My Fire" confronted the Doors with a new dilemma: whether to keep transforming the song or quit playing it altogether.

Morrison in particular now came to loathe "Light My Fire." At a December 1968 concert, when the audience began hurling lit matches and calling for the song, Morrison yelled at them to "cut out that shit."[39] In early 1969 he told an interviewer that the Doors wouldn't perform the song in public again, explaining that "it stinks. We're beyond that now."[40] Of course, they did perform the song many times that year, including the infamous Miami performance, 1 March 69, where he used the solo section as an occasion to cajole the audience into coming onstage and dancing.[41] As Krieger played his solo, Morrison squatted down with his head close to the body of the guitar—prompting his arrest on the charge that he had publicly simulated fellatio. At the trial his attorney questioned him: "During the time that [Krieger] was taking that solo run on his guitar [in "Light My Fire"], what did you do, if anything?" Morrison replied, "I got down on my hands and knees and scrutinized the intricate finger movements of the guitar player." When asked why he did that, Morrison said, "I don't play the guitar and it amazes me how someone is able to do it. It is *masterful.*"[42] Despite his testimony, Morrison was convicted.

Shortly thereafter the Doors abandoned the song's strategic place in the program, usually relegating "Light My Fire" to an encore.[43] In June, the group omitted the song entirely from their Chicago concert, only to have the emcee call them back to the stage, insisting that no Doors concert would be complete without "Light My Fire."[44] At a January 1970 concert, Morrison introduced it by telling the audience dryly that the group was going to play "a famous radio song."[45] The group's ambivalence toward "Light My Fire" showed in their renditions, which were alternately passionate and listless—even from one night to the next.[46]

Nevertheless, they kept trying new variations, as if to continually reclaim the song for themselves.[47] For his part, Morrison began to preface "Light My Fire" with a recitation, borrowed from the opening to *The Soft Parade* album (released in the fall of 1969): "When I was back there in seminary school, there was a person there who put forth the proposition that you can petition the Lord with prayer . . . petition the Lord with prayer . . . petition the Lord with prayer. [screaming] *You cannot petition the Lord with prayer!*" He also continued to alter the melody, stripping it down more severely than ever. At various times he sang the first verse entirely on the note C and the chorus entirely on A or D; sang the second and fourth verses down a perfect fourth from the first and third; substituted short new melodic ideas, as though the song were a blues or gospel tune. Moreover, he distorted the timbre of his voice. In the studio version Morrison had crooned the melody in what one writer called "his best Elvis Presley voice."[48] Now he sometimes exaggerated the style until it parodied lounge-singing; feigned a raspy/gravelly soul style; delivered the vocal in speech-song; or sang in a completely nondescript, soulless voice, as though disembodied. It is difficult to say how much these variations resulted from his increasing use of alcohol, his desire to keep the song interesting to perform, or both.

Meanwhile, Manzarek, Krieger, and Densmore played the solo section much as they had before, but continued to expand its proportions. Manzarek played more ferociously, yet followed the same pattern as in 1967–68. Krieger kept the basic architecture of the studio solo, including the motivic and registral signposts. But between them he played in an increasingly collage-like fashion, moving freely among blues and jazz licks, pseudo-Middle-Eastern embellishments, and dorian or aeolian mode quotations ranging from "Eleanor Rigby" and other recent hits to "My Favorite Things" itself. The subsections after the guitar solo remained more or less as they had been. On at least one occasion, though, the players used this portion of the song to quote the musical opening to "When the Music's Over," just as Morrison had quoted its text in many earlier performances.[49] And Morrison found even more ways to participate in the solo section. For example, before or after the guitar solo he began to quote the lyrics to three old pop standards—"Summertime," "St. James Infirmary," and "Fever." (These standards connected to the solo section and to each other through their minor keys/modes as well as their allusions to temperature.) Morrison sometimes even played harmonica during the responsorial passage, allowing him an actual place in the instrumental improvisation.

Their rendition of "Light My Fire" in Vancouver, June 1970, was a kind of consummation. In this performance, the proportions of the song grew to their largest recorded dimensions (Figure 2c). Yet there is neither a contrapuntal duo nor a responsorial trio. Instead, the players insert the appropriate chord changes during Morrison's long recitations: one verse from "Summertime," one from "St. James Infirmary," two verses from "Fever," and the hypnotic repetition of the line "Everybody's got the fever." This version was perhaps their most important musical manifesto about the song: after a long love-hate relationship, they acknowledged what everyone else knew—the song was both essential and trivial. As its creators they had to keep it as a part of their repertoire, but they also had to treat it like a cover version. Beginning as a distinctly innovative work, "Light My Fire" had joined its minor-key pop predecessors in a musical pantheon that existed primarily to make medleys.

Fittingly, "Light My Fire" turned out to be the last song all four members of the Doors performed together. At the Warehouse in New Orleans, 12 December 1970, a drunken Morrison sat down in front of the drums during the solos but refused to get up and cue the retransition. The instrumentalists kept playing until Densmore finally kicked Morrison, who went to the mikestand, rammed it down through the stage and walked off. Densmore said "that's it" and threw his drumsticks down, leaving the stage to Manzarek and Krieger.[50]

*

After Morrison's death in the summer of 1971 Manzarek, Krieger, and Densmore reunited to play occasional concerts featuring Manzarek (or other singers) on vocals and even audience singalongs of "Light My Fire." They released two post-Morrison albums, *Other Voices* (1971) and *Full Circle* (1972), before breaking up entirely. One of their last acts together was to agree to sell "Light My Fire" to Tiparillo, who, like Buick, wanted it for a commercial jingle. Morrison's common-law widow, Pamela Courson, vetoed the plan.[51]

Once separated, Manzarek and Krieger—the two members of the group who had used the song as a vehicle for solos—tried to keep a quasi-Doors version of "Light My Fire" in their repertoire. In the 1970s Manzarek played the song with his new group, Nite City, featuring Iggy Pop on vocals. Krieger continued playing the song through the 1990s, using various singers and backup bands. They played it true to form.

Meanwhile, pop groups continued to rehash the post-Feliciano "Light My Fire" in whatever was the fashion of the moment. In the late 1970s disco versions appeared, all of which, of course, set the music to a thumping dance beat. One artist even made a disco sequel, unblushingly titled "Relight My Fire."[52]

In early 1993, when the Doors were inducted into the Rock and Roll Hall of Fame, Manzarek, Krieger, and Densmore reunited to perform the song with Pearl Jam's lead singer Eddie Vedder. While staying fairly true to the original song, Vedder provided one more footnote to the song's evolution: he corrected the grammar, singing "you know that I would be a liar / If I *were* to say to you, / Girl, we couldn't get much higher."

But "Light My Fire" had long since come full circle: it had become "My Favorite Things." When "My Favorite Things" inspired the Doors' first hit, it was already far from the Rodgers and Hammerstein song originally meant to illuminate the character of Sister Maria in *The Sound of Music*. It was a set of musical trappings in which to experiment, a pretext for improvisation. Just so with "Light My Fire." One could willfully play with it, as the Doors did, making it a repository for fragments of songs by artists ranging from Gershwin to the Beatles as well as self-quotations from "When the Music's Over" and "The End." Or one could, as many did, reduce it to a simple post–Tin Pan Alley tune, at once instantly recognizable and immediately disposable.

The fate of "Light My Fire" reveals clearly the inevitable tension between artistic intent and the mass market. By 1967 the society at large had embraced the superficialities of anything "psychedelic"—including the music. Most rock groups hoped to make it big in "show business," yet retain their status as outsiders. A hit song could elevate a group financially but doom it artistically. As the mass market adopted and embraced the bare-bones version of "Light My Fire," the Doors fought to keep their version distinct, emphasizing and embellishing those aspects of the song that pop culture discarded. But eventually even the Doors played with "Fire" in ways that seemed to admit that the song's success had consumed it.

7 Ends and Means

The psychedelic aesthetic led rock musicians to dynamize one of the fundamental parts of a song's form—its ending. In countless recordings of the late 1960s, rock groups tried new ways of complicating the moments just before the sound stopped. In doing so, they often turned the ending of a song into its most striking feature.[1]

How to end a rock song had always posed a problem. The music usually had a fierce rhythmic momentum but no large-scale harmonic drive. The traditional cadential formulae of western music could hardly be effective in rock, since I, IV, and V chords had become the stuff of harmonic oscillations and tiny, repetitive gestures. Rock had little other harmonic vocabulary by which to punctuate its forms. To deal with both the rhythmic momentum and the harmonic stasis, rock musicians at first turned to two different types of ending. In concert, players freely prolonged the final chord, not only applying a fermata to it, but improvising over it, rapidly reattacking it, and embellishing it with scalar passage work and drum and cymbal rolls—until the group leader cued one final attack. Derived from jazz and rhythm and blues, this technique dramatized the end of what was otherwise a relatively static formal design. It also dispersed the rhythmic momentum, like a valve relieving built-up pressure. The studio, however, afforded a better solution: the recording engineer could "fade" the recording, slowly turning down the levels while the performers repeated some part of the song's form.

It was almost inadvertent that the fade became the standard way to end a record. For decades recordings of classical pieces rarely fit onto one side of a 78-rpm record; a Beethoven sonata, for example, might require six sides or more. Rather than chop movements into segments that would fit, the recording engineer would fade a movement out on one side of the record, and fade it back in on the other side. If a movement could not be completed on two sides (about three minutes each), it would fade out again on the second side, fade in again on the next record, and so on, until it was finished. This was a plausible response to the dilemma of avoiding long pieces or abruptly stopping the flow of music. In the mid-1940s, some jazz artists used fades on records of live concerts.[2] This worked a little better, perhaps, than fades on classical records, since the engineers could fade between solos, minimizing the disruption of flow.

It was not until 1946 that a complete recording actually ended with a fade. "Open the Door, Richard," by Jack McVea and His All Stars, was a novelty recording of a minstrel-style routine. The humor of the routine depended on the seemingly endless pounding of a drunken man on Richard's door, with the band members singing a refrain that calls for Richard to open the door. This recording faded at the end, making it seem that "the audience [was] getting weary and leaving Richard's hapless buddies standing out on the street, shouting and pounding. . . . We turn the corner and they're gone."[3] Within a few years non-novelty recordings adopted the technique; soon it became the normal and expected way of ending a pop song in the studio.[4]

The fade redefined what an ending could be. It did not really end in the conventional sense. Instead, it seemed to transport the song to some remote distance beyond the listener's range of hearing. Unlike a final cadence, the fade dispersed the rhythmic momentum of a rock song by dissipating its dynamic energy. By allowing for more repetitions of the "hook"—the most important structural segment—the fade could also make a song more memorable and perhaps even more likeable.[5] Since no new musical information appeared in the moments before the sound stopped, the fade also gave radio announcers more space for commercials and patter. As it turned out, announcers began to treat non-fade endings in the same way. The "real" end of the song no longer mattered.

As psychedelic ideals permeated music, rock artists formulated new ways of ending, as if to dramatize their loftier artistic goals. They did not completely abandon the basic techniques of final cadence or fade—after all, the music still had to stop at some point.[6] But they began to find means to intensify the moments just before a song stopped playing. In retrospect, all of these endings relied on four distinct techniques: (1) lamination, (2) delamination, (3) resumption, and (4) substitution. We will consider these one by one, as separate devices; afterwards we will be able to see how they combined into more complex endings.

*

In *lamination* rock artists superimposed layers of new, contrasting material onto the existing closing material. Because lamination usually required extra performers or technological resources, the best examples come from the most prominent groups—above all the Beatles, who in a single year laminated the endings of five songs, each in a very different way. In February 1967, John Lennon wanted to create a circus-like atmosphere for "Being for the Benefit of Mr. Kite," one of the tracks on *Sgt. Pepper's Lonely Hearts Club Band.* To do this George Martin made a sonic collage of calliope music and sound effects, superimposing it onto the basic tracks of the recording in the middle and the end. In the first case, he kept it relatively faint, blending it into the total mix. But when he repeated it, he made it dominate the texture until the song's abrupt end.[7] That same month the Beatles recorded the monumental "A Day in the Life," which also contained laminated sections in both the middle and the end. The acetate of the song shows that the group originally had no definite plan for these segments of the recording. In both of them road manager Mal Evans audibly counts off twenty-four measures, while Paul McCartney plays increasingly complex piano harmonies, eventually arriving at loud random chords above florid bass lines.[8] McCartney decided to superimpose four takes of an aleatory orchestral sound mass onto both of these twenty-four-measure segments. Initially, the second orchestral mass ended the song.[9] Later the group tried attaching more conventional endings to it, including the definitive one: the famous three-piano E-major chord.[10]

Later that year they laminated the endings of three other recordings. In the last forty-four seconds of "Good Morning, Good Morning" they superimposed a series of animal noises, each noise representing an animal capable of devouring the one preceding it. They laminated the last full minute of "I Am the Walrus" with random radio feeds from the BBC—primarily test signals and spoken voice tracks from a production of *King Lear.*[11] For "All You Need Is Love" they created perhaps their most memorable laminated ending. Onto a long vocal/instrumental vamp (on the words "love is all you need") they collaged fragments of several other musical works. The first two fragments are played in the key and tempo of the song itself (G major, ♩ = 107): Bach's Two-Part Invention no. 8 (in the trumpets) and Glenn Miller's "In the Mood" (in the tenor saxophones).[12] Then the violins play "Greensleeves" in the relative minor key at a much slower tempo (E minor, ♩=ca. 30).[13] Finally, John Lennon sings "she loves you, yeah, yeah, yeah" twice (in G).[14] The BBC described the final product as "not just a single performance but a whole montage of performances."[15]

Most artists, lacking the Beatles' resources, had to settle for simpler kinds of lamination: slight layerings of human speech, sound effects, or processed instrumental sound. In "Purple Haze" (1967), for example, Jimi Hendrix laminates his ending by applying ring modulation to his solo guitar, then adding a slowed-down recording of his voice uttering the song title; these two new layers continue through the fade to the end of the recording. In "The Unknown Soldier" (1968), the Doors use similar methods to illustrate the closing words of the song ("war is over"). They add a delay effect to the organ, then superimpose the sound of steeple chimes, followed by crowd noises. One could also superimpose backtracked layers of recorded material already present in the song. As mentioned in chapter 5, the Beatles had superimposed a reversed portion of "Rain" (1966) onto its fade. The Monkees did similarly in the fade to "Pleasant Valley Sunday" (1967): backwards fragments of the guitar tracks swell and recede against the repetitions of the words "another Pleasant Valley Sunday."[16]

Lamination certainly connoted psychedelic experience: LSD users observed that the drug made music acquire "layered levels of sound."[17] But lamination also opened up a song, making it a prism of its environment. If psychedelic artists complicated the horizontal form of a song, they also used lamination to diversify the vertical texture. Without lamination, fading repetitions tended to weaken a song through inertia, make it seem to get stuck on itself. Lamination provided fresh ideas to thicken and embellish the music at its close. The new layers made energy from friction as they rubbed up against each other.[18] Just when a song was "supposed" to collapse into itself, it began to pull other worlds into its orbit—radio dramas, animal sounds, or even transformed echoes of itself.

Delamination did the opposite: the rock musicians gradually (or abruptly) stripped away layers already present in the recording. Of course, this was much easier than lamination. It also seemed "natural," rooted in the varying characteristics of the instruments. When a rock song ended with a simple cadence the sound of each instrument decayed at a different rate. A cymbal rang longer than the rhythm guitar, which normally rang longer than the bass; an organ, having no decay, had to cut off. Delamination toyed with this principle: the organist, for example, might simply sustain the sound longer than the other instruments, or the fuzz-tone guitar (as in Pride and Joy's "If You're Ready," 1967) play as much as nine seconds after the other instruments drop out.

In recording a song that would end with a fade, players normally vamped for awhile then stopped one at a time, haphazardly dismantling the texture. Or, knowing that a fade would come sometime before they stopped playing, instrumentalists would often accelerate or decelerate and improvise some final licks before actually stopping. That is, each player found his or her own way of dispersing the momentum of the song. In delamination one could actually hear them doing so. Near the end of Love's "Laughing Stock" (1968), the players gradually desynchronize, then stop more or less simultaneously—except for the bassist, who continues playing for two more seconds. What one hears in this recording is the loose sort of ending that would often be *performed* in the studio, but not *heard* on the record, because a fade would have preceded it.

Some delaminations by Jimi Hendrix should be heard as sequels to that practice. In his "Love or Confusion" (1967) the bass stops first, the drums two seconds later, and the guitar five seconds after that; in "Still Raining, Still Dreaming" (1968) three seconds separate the organ cut off from the subsequent cymbal dampening, with the wah-wah guitar playing solo for three more seconds (finally cut off by a brief, distant shout). But delamination could be much longer, allowing a solo instrument— usually the lead guitar—to play a kind of codetta. The Rolling Stones' "Have You Seen Your Mother, Baby, Standing in the Shadow?" (1966) appears to end with an abrupt cadence of all the instruments at 2:20. But the fuzztone guitar continues to play solo for an additional thirteen seconds, ending with its own cadence. In Hendrix's "House Burning Down" (1968), the rhythm section ceases, but Hendrix plays past their ending for twenty-eight seconds, using extended techniques to create an engine sound (and pseudo-doppler effect). Here the delamination has poetic intent: it portrays the arrival of motorcycles at the scene of an arson.[19]

Although the Beatles may have been the first to delaminate an ending, they used the technique sparingly. They constructed "Tomorrow Never Knows" (1966) from a vocal track, a rhythm track, and tape loops of sped-up guitar sounds, a honky-tonk piano, and so forth. At the end of the song, they stop the rhythm track and tape loops completely independently, allowing the whole texture to simply unravel. Thereafter, the group abandoned this way of ending except in two songs, both on the so-called White Album (1968). "The Continuing Adventures of Bungalow Bill" dissipates all of the instruments in the texture except for a lone mellotron (sounding like a bassoon) that plays seven measures of the chorus in swing style over the sound of a small group applauding. Meanwhile, "Don't Pass Me By" ends with a solo fiddle playing the same country fills that had appeared in breaks between the chorus and verse.

Unlike the fade, delamination did not suggest that the music was continuing inaudibly in some remote domain. If anything, it demystified the music, exposing one or more of its discrete parts, as if by evisceration.[20] And in a few cases it may have had extra connotations—consider Sly and the Family Stone's "Dance to the Music" (1968). Borrowing an old rhythm-and-blues technique, the song introduces instrumental layers gradually (drums, lead guitar, bass, organ, horns). But near the end the horns and drums fade out, leaving the bass, lead guitar, and a solo soprano sax to play contrapuntal licks as a trio for the last nine seconds. In this case the delamination seems to reverse the progressive layering found earlier in the song.

In *resumption* the music ostensibly ends then begins again before the "real" end. This technique obviously derived from the old reprise or "one more time" tradition of extending a song.[21] In fact, some resumptions simply modified that device. After what appears to be the end of "Piggies" (1968), for example, the Beatles actually say "one more time," then attach an embellished plagal cadence—but in a key three whole steps lower (ending on what becomes the V of the following song). Similarly, Hendrix ostensibly ends "Bold As Love" (1968) with an emphatic plagal cadence (two measures apiece of IV and I in A♭ major, played three times). Suddenly the song resumes with a drum solo and an instrumental reprise of the song, but one whole step higher than the rest of the song.

Other resumptions used the fade. This practice descends from two earlier songs: the Contours' "Do You Love Me?" (1962) and the Gentrys' "Keep On Dancing" (1965). The Contours fade out for six seconds, as if to end the song, then suddenly fade *back in* on the words "work, work." (The "real" fade ending ensues eighteen seconds later).[22] The original recording of "Keep On Dancing" faded from 1:22–1:31, leaving the song too short to be marketable. So the group spliced a dub of the original recording onto the end of the fade, creating a very literal reprise (which fades all over again at 2:02–2:09). As it turned out, this reprise actually supports the text: "*keep on* dancing."

Hendrix and the Beatles used fade-resumptions that were, respectively, less and more elaborate than those of their rock 'n' roll precursors. Hendrix uses very short resumptions in two songs: in "Manic Depression" (1967) the instruments fade, but the cymbal rapidly fades back in for two more seconds; similarly, in "Are You Experienced?" (1967), the guitar fades back in after the other instruments leave and reverberates for six more seconds.[23] The Beatles, on the other hand, expand the idea of resumption in "Helter Skelter" (1968).[24] Since the best takes of this song were far too long to appear on an album—one was twenty-seven minutes—the group in effect invites the listener to "revisit" the song in various states of progress marked by two separate fades (out by 3:42, then back in, then nearly out again at 4:17, then back in for a final cadential gesture, including Ringo's explosive shout "I've got blisters on my fingers!"). In this last case, resumption resembles the cinematic technique of fading out and in on the same scene in order to show the passage of huge lengths of time.

But resumption also enhances any song's sense of energy. The technique implies that a mere fade is not enough to quell the song's power; some latent energy in the song seems to overwhelm the first attempt to contain it. Nevertheless, resumption is a technique so blatant and easy to accomplish that it apparently became a rather unsatisfying mannerism, using up its freshness in just a few recordings.

The fourth and most complex technique is *substitution,* where the artists end with material completely different from the rest of the music that precedes it. In the early 1960s engine sounds ended some hot-rod songs (e.g., Conny and the Bellhops' "Shot Rod," 1960) and the sounds of ocean waves ended some surf instrumentals (e.g., the Chantays' "Pipeline," 1963). In such cases the sound effects generally had appeared earlier in the song. In recordings of the late 1960s, however, the artists added utterly new, unexpected sounds at a song's end. Thus, Buffalo Springfield ends "Broken Arrow" (1967) with a solo heartbeat; and the Beatles conclude "I'm So Tired" (1968) with a muttering voice trailing off as if into sleep. Primitive substitutions such as these neutralize the momentum of the song by shifting the focus to some literal transcription of "reality." They also show a willingness to incorporate "noise" into "music"—a well-known trait of twentieth-century music. Still, no matter how much they pervade recordings of the late 1960s, these kinds of substitutions do not differ in essence from those of earlier recordings.

But some of the most impressive endings in the 1960s juxtapose contrasting *instrumental music* with the main body of the song. Love pioneered this kind of substitution in "Seven and Seven Is" (1966). The main body of the song is in the key of A (alternating A major and A minor), fast ($\downarrow$ = 155), with subdivisions of the beat strongly articulated by the drums.[25] At what appears to be the end Love superimposes onto the dominant (E-minor) chord a recording of a nuclear test blast—seemingly a simple sound-effects substitution. But in its aftermath they play an instrumental coda—a slow dance in C major, with compound-meter ($\downarrow$ = 52) and a generic doo-wop harmonic progression (I-vi-IV-V) unlike anything earlier in the song. This new music fades over the next twenty seconds.

In 1967–68 the Beatles used substitutions for the endings of three songs. The first was in "Aerial Tour Instrumental," an early version of what became "Flying" in the soundtrack to *Magical Mystery Tour* (1967). The group ostensibly ends the song—basically a slow twelve-bar blues—with a cadence after a mere minute and a half. They then attach a recording of two choruses of a fast, 1920s-style twelve-bar blues, pitched a major third lower and played on different instruments.[26] They use a much more dramatic substitution at the end of "Glass Onion" (1968). The body of the song is moderately fast ($\downarrow$ = 122) and dominated by fuzz guitars. After the half cadence that ends the final chorus the group attaches a recording of a tritone-laden ostinato, much slower ($\downarrow$ = 91) and played by a string quartet (which gradually slows and fades). Unlike the stylistic substitution that concludes "Aerial Tour Instrumental," this substitution encompasses the complete content—pitch, rhythm, and timbre.

The Beatles tried two alternate substitutions for the end of "Cry Baby Cry" (1968). On his demo for this song Lennon changed the meter in the final chorus from simple to compound, while keeping the division of the beat constant.[27] The substitution of one manner for another resembles that of "Aerial Tour Instrumental," but Lennon discarded it before the final version. That final version ends instead with a song fragment by McCartney (words: "can you take me back where I came from, can you take me back?"). The harmony of this ending consists of a single, reiterated chord, a half-step above the rest of "Cry Baby Cry."[28] Although the pulse and acoustic accompaniment of the fragment resemble those of the song that precedes it, no other similarities link the two.

Substitution replaces a song's kinetic energy with the energy of juxta-position, requiring the listener to find connections between the seemingly unconnected. Thus, substitution changes the problem of dispersing momentum into a problem of reconciling foreign entities—one longer and weightier, the other shorter and more trivial. The technique also delegates the real task of ending to the shorter idea—which can end more easily because it lacks the mass and momentum of the song proper.

The four types of endings we have discussed divide into two aesthetic pairs. The collage technique of lamination superimposes vertically on a spatial plane; the montage technique of substitution juxtaposes laterally on a temporal plane. But both depend on what film theorist Sergei Eisenstein called "the conflict of two pieces in opposition to each other," creating a "collision" of ideas.[29] Delamination brings the randomness behind fades into the listener's ear; resumption plays with the listener's expectations of what a fade connotes. Both exploit the conventions of rock records. All four techniques arise directly from the uniqueness of the recording medium, the ability to layer tracks, to splice pieces of tape, to turn volume knobs up or down. These new types of endings confirm that rock had moved from performance art to studio art. It existed (for the time being) more on records than on concert stages.

Of course, the four basic types of ending only begin to encompass the rich variety of new endings that appeared. Many endings defied neat categorization. For example, the Rolling Stones' "We Love You" (1967) fades out then back in, but with a transposed, highly distorted take of the vocal track to the song—not quite resumption, not quite substitution. Other recordings combined techniques such as lamination and delamination, introducing some *new* layer near the end of a song then stripping away the *old* layers, leaving only the new layer to finish the track. The Beatles' sound-effects endings often overlap in just this way: the blackbird calls at the end of "Blackbird," the jet airplane sounds in "Back in the USSR," and the pig noises that overlap with the "one more time" ending of "Piggies" (all from 1968). Such overlapping could appear in instrumental contexts as well: in "If 6 Was 9" (1967), Hendrix superimposes improvisatory soprano recorder licks onto the final guitar solo, then removes everything but those licks. One could even combine lamination/delamination with substitution, as the Beatles did in the final version of "Flying" (1967). First, all the instruments but the mellotron drop out—evidently a delamination. Then the group superimposes a backwards recording of the mellotron onto itself—lamination. Both mellotrons, the forward and the backward, continue playing, but music so different in character from the main body of the song as to suggest substitution.

Moreover, as we have seen, the initial idea of an ending and its final realization did not always correspond. The Beatles' "Strawberry Fields Forever" (1967) involved many takes and, eventually, the splicing together of two completely different arrangements—one sped up from its original form, the other slowed down. The ending of the final version is well known: following the final chorus, the instrumental vamp gradually fades out, then a strange, seemingly unrelated music fades in, with a mellotron tape loop (sounding like flutes) in the foreground. Tim Riley describes it this way: "After the fade-out a new set of wandering noises comes back in: a snare drum marches judiciously onward; flutes flicker and sputter around a repetitive guitar note."[30] On the surface this appears to be a substitution.

But the tape master of remix twenty-six, from which the final version was made, shows that the mellotron tape loop actually began as a lamination onto the existing vamp. (In fact, the group had tried the same effect with a different loop—of horns—in remix twenty-five). Why the fade out and subsequent fade in? Drummer Ringo Starr gets off the beat, apparently when someone briefly converses with him during that portion of the recording. Within a few seconds he gets back on the beat, remaining there for the duration of the take. In the final mix, to expunge the drumming error, the song fades out for the few awkward offbeat seconds and fades back in as Starr returns to the beat. Coincidentally, the mellotron loop begins at the same point. Thus, this rather serendipitous ending began as a lamination, added a resumption (to cover mistakes), but ultimately sounds like a substitution.

The four types of ending and their hybrids became so common that conventional endings grew passé. Rock artists either found special kinds of endings or avoided ending altogether. As the Beatles and other groups began to think of records in terms of albums rather than singles, many of them elided their songs, devising *transitions* rather than endings. And as we saw in connection with psychedelic rock, some California groups transferred that avoidance of endings into their live performances. The performances became medleys, collections of songs that ran one into another without a break.[31]

For their final album, *Abbey Road* (1969), the Beatles composed two fitting postscripts to the whole obsession with new endings. During the final remix of the last song on the first side of the album, "I Want You (She's So Heavy)," Alan Parsons recalls that, "we were listening to the mix [and] John said 'There! Cut the tape there.' Geoff [Emerick] cut the tape and that was it"—twenty seconds before the actual ending of the take.[32] Thus, the recording simply stops without preparation, literally clipped off. Tim Riley aptly describes it as a "sudden-death effect . . . as though the needle has jumped off the vinyl."[33]

On the second side of the album, the group had constructed a huge medley of songs, ending with a brief one simply titled "The End." After the basic tracks were recorded, McCartney decided that "Her Majesty," one of the songs in the medley, was weak. He had engineer John Kurlander remove it and cover the edit with instrumental overdubs. Trained never to throw anything away, Kurlander attached "Her Majesty" to the end of the album's master tape. By accident, the song became the actual ending of the record. Ironically, the final chord of "Her Majesty" was missing, inadvertently left buried in the medley mix.[34]

The endings of the two sides of *Abbey Road*—one arbitrary, the other accidental—seem to shrug off the elaborate techniques that the Beatles and others had worked so hard to develop. On the first side Lennon intuitively ends the song, neither evading nor solving the problem of ending, but simply negating it. The fortunate accident that ended the second side creates a radical, but wholly unpremeditated new ending. It reaffirmed that in art the inadvertent sometimes transforms itself into the inevitable. The endings of both sides of *Abbey Road* seemed to say that the pursuit of elaborate techniques for ending had become tiresome and moot: the ends questioned the means. And by relying on the sudden and the circumstantial, they conjured up the irrepressible, fundamentally playful spirit with which rock 'n' roll itself had begun.

Appendix 1: Sources

As academics continue to delve into rock, their students might be tempted to rely on a set of standard writings on the subject, sources that fit tidily into a conventional bibliography with the usual categories (books, articles, theses, dissertations). This book, however, builds on the premise that the means to grasping rock should be as unruly as the music itself. In what follows I want to discuss the kinds of sources that I relied on and comment on what other rock scholars have done.

*

In orthodox musicology one should study scores. In rock musicology one should study records. Although published rock "scores" (i.e., sheet music) exist, they almost invariably consist of bare-boned attempts to transcribe harmonies and melodies, without conveying a sense of a recording's ambient timbres or its spatial presence. Rock musicians preserve their music in recordings; rock sheet music is an afterthought, one that almost transgresses the aural foundations of the art.[1] The problem with rock sheet music, or rock transcriptions, is one that ethnomusicologists have encountered for decades—how can one rightly notate a music that is composed and transmitted orally and aurally?[2]

Most of the rock music mentioned in this book appears on easily accessible mainstream record labels in a variety of formats—vinyl, cassette, compact disc, and so forth. If a scholar wants to study matters such as harmony and form, any format will suffice. But to comprehend the *heard sonorities* of mid- to late-1960s rock, the scholar really needs to hear vinyl records, the format of that time period.[3] (It need not be pristine vinyl, since, as I suggested earlier, the grainy sound of slightly degraded vinyl is, often as not, what people actually *heard*). If vinyl is unavailable, tapes are usable, but have a hiss that obscures the subtleties of even intentionally distorted sounds. Compact discs best facilitate the repeated study of specific moments of music. But they are in many respects undesirable, differing considerably in balance and overall ambience from both tape and vinyl—the "blend" of the original recordings is usually missing, the instruments sound more discrete and aloof (although higher sampling rates should help this in the future). Compact discs also often contain new recording mixes foreign to the original records. After weighing the various options, one should proceed, studying the monophonic versions of records originally conceived as such—normal into at least 1967 (even though stereo versions exist prior to that date). Likewise, one should study the stereo versions of records specifically designed for that format.

Many of the lesser-known titles mentioned in this book were accessible to me only through compilation albums, some on vinyl and others on compact discs. Such compilation albums allow students of a style access to many songs otherwise too obscure (and thus hard-to-find and expensive) to collect for research.

It was just such a compilation album that inspired the musicians who created "punk rock" in the mid-1970s. Armed with one of the new technologies of the day—a cassette tape recorder—Elektra Records founder Jac Holzman began making his own private compilations of rock songs in about 1971, tape anthologies of "all those tracks from albums that had one good track on them."[4] Thinking such an anthology would make a good album, Holzman asked Lenny Kaye to make his own selection. The result was the double album compilation *Nuggets: Original Artyfacts from the First Psychedelic Era, 1965–1968,* which featured twenty-seven recordings, some well-known, others little-known, most of them raucous exemplars of what would later be known as garage rock. Many listeners seized upon these recordings as alternatives to the prevailing "progressive rock" of the day.

Countless compilation albums imitated the *Nuggets* format, including Rhino Records' later *Nuggets* series and perhaps the best-known long-running anthology of cult-classic obscurities, Archive International Productions' *Pebbles.* The little-known recordings mentioned in this book may be found on dozens of compilation albums of the post-*Nuggets* sort, albums indexed in David Walters's essential reference work on the subject, *The Children of Nuggets*.[5] But the rock scholar should be aware that new collections of reissued garage rock obscurities appear with increasing frequency, many of them on ad hoc record labels not meant to outlast two or three titles. Since these reissues of rare records are so profuse and so ephemeral, the serious scholar of the style needs to keep alert to their appearance and build his or her own archive on a regular basis (at no small cost).

Any serious rock scholar must also contend with an indispensable but precarious archive: bootleg recordings. Bootleg records, audio or video tapes, and compact discs are (usually) unlicensed dubs of recording sessions, alternate takes, and live performances. The recordings on some bootlegs were made by the artists' own record labels. But they remained unissued by the labels and, for most scholars, are extraordinarily hard to examine through other means (such as researching the companies' tape archives). Most live-performance recordings were made by concert audio engineers or members of the audience. They often circulate through networks of tape traders, many of whom constantly pursue a better dub (a tape copy closer to the original recording).

Often illegal to sell—but not to buy (as of this writing)—bootlegs have a cloudy legal status. Yet few rock scholars can afford to neglect such a resource. Bootleg recordings can document the evolution of rock songs in the same way as drafts of literary works or sketches of visual art. They show the real breadth of the rock artistic enterprise. Moreover, they prevent the artists or their recording companies from defining their artistic process without confirmatory documentation. As Lenny Kaye puts it, bootlegs keep the music "out of not only the industry's conception of the artist, but also the artist's conception of the artist."[6] By documenting the details of rock songs' evolution and performance practice, bootlegs remind scholars that rock "is about 'the moment,' that you might have to wade through [much inferior material] to find one clear moment, but no record company can capture each and every one worth preserving."[7]

The first step to take in rock scholarship, then, is to listen to as many recordings as is feasible. Then the scholar can let the educated ear guide him or her into what seems most notable in the music. Along the way—but not too prematurely—one should read what other listeners and scholars have had to say.

Most writers about rock during the last thirty years treat lyrics as the real locus of the art—an art that is primarily, as one author puts it, "a sensitive gauge of public attitudes [and] an excellent exploratory device for making judgments about modern life."[8] Rock is music with a "message"—so goes the assumption—a message that is legible on the semantic surface of the song and (at best) illuminated by the underlying tonal/rhythmic structures and vocal delivery. Many books and articles treat rock as a special form of poetry, polemic, or political discourse. Although this kind of rock scholarship is beginning to wane, some recent scholarly works continue to foster it. Robert Patison, for example, in a recent book purporting to examine "rock music" focuses almost exclusively on rock lyrics. (He acknowledges that to do more would belie his own "very limited musical competence.")[9] In his more recent book, James Harris makes the extraordinary claim that his work "breaks new ground by concentrating on a facet of rock music which has received far too little attention: the intellectual themes, preoccupations, and even arguments, to be found in the lyrics of rock songs"—as if that were not the preeminent object of study in rock scholarship since the 1960s.[10]

Studying the words is valuable, of course, since so long as one is listening to *songs,* the lyrics matter—even if the function of the singing is sometimes to confound the words. Yet it is rock's tendency to obfuscate words that matters more. Susan McClary and Robert Walser rightly critique the conventional modus operandi of analyzing rock songs, noting that much rock is neither constructed nor received primarily around a text, and that in some cases "obscurity of the verbal dimension seems even to be part of the attraction."[11] David Byrne (of Talking Heads) explains the relationship of words to music in rock from an autobiographical perspective: "When I grew up and first started hearing rock music . . . it was the *sound* that really struck me. The words were, for the most part, pretty stupid." He goes on to say that it was the musical "texture" that outweighed the words or even the melody line, because "The texture a group of musicians arrives at. . . . can make a statement that supports or contradicts [the lyrics]."[12]

Recently, more scholars have begun to investigate the specifically musical traits of various rock styles. This new wave—indeed, flood—of rock scholarship typically combines conventional musical analytical techniques with methods of interpreting the *meaning* of those techniques, whether through fresh modes of analysis (e.g., semiotic analysis) or new critical lenses (e.g., gender studies). Recent books probably succeed best when the music they treat fits into some readily identifiable subcategory of rock that borrows heavily from classical traditions—such as heavy metal (see Robert Walser's *Running with the Devil: Power, Gender, and Madness in Heavy Metal Music*) or progressive rock (see Edward Macan's *Rocking the Classics: English Progressive Rock and the Counterculture*). More ambitious but harder to evaluate are books that try to create paradigms for *all* forms of rock from the 1950s to the present (see Allan Moore's *Rock, the Primary Text*, or Theodore Gracyk's more focused *Rhythm and Noise: An Aesthetics of Rock*) or even paradigms that work for all forms of popular music itself, including rock. Among this latter type are Richard Middleton's *Studying Popular Music* and David Brackett's *Interpreting Popular Music*, which range rather freely among semiotic, spectral, Schenkerian, and other modes of structural analysis in order to unravel the aesthetic "codes" that run through popular music from Bing Crosby to Elvis Costello and seemingly every popular artist before, after, and in between.

In discussing the voice in popular music, scholars routinely invoke Roland Barthes's idea of "the grain of the voice."[13] Barthes argues that singing should be analyzed and evaluated according to the unique characteristics of the individual voice ("geno-song") rather than according to its faithfulness to various traditions or to codes of stylistic correctness ("pheno-song").[14] Simon Frith assesses the "grain" concept in this somewhat overstated way: "We enjoy hearing someone sing not because they are expressing something else, not because the voice represents the 'person' behind it, but because the voice, as a sound in itself, has an immediate voluptuous appeal."[15] In other words, it should be appreciated not on a semantic or psychological level, but on a purely sensuous one. The voice must be described, although not with a systematic jargon—as Barthes said in an interview: "The *grain* of the voice is not indescribable (nothing is indescribable), but I don't think that it can be defined scientifically"; one describes it "only through metaphors."[16]

But Barthes's "grain" idea should not be canonized. So far, the writings spawned by it generally suffer from two problems. First, they tend to use mere adjective-laden descriptions of a given voice's special qualities in terms essentially no different from those of rock journalism. Second, they tend to neglect certain recurring traits of rock singing, overlooking the traditions and codes of vocal behavior that actually exist in rock. Consider, for example, these remarks by Frith about Elvis Presley: "in the end . . . the only way we can explain his appeal [is] not in terms of what he 'stood for,' socially or personally, but by reference to the *grain* of his voice. Elvis Presley's music was thrilling because it dissolved the signs that had previously put adolescence together. He celebrated—more sensually, more voluptuously than any other rock 'n' roll singer—the act of symbol creation itself."[17]

All of this may be true. But it does not tell us very much about what made Presley's singing work. It is as though in describing the grain of a specific piece of oak one were to say that it "inspired the craft of beautiful cabinet making." Even if true, that statement conveys no sense of what that grain looks like, what complex of lines, shades, and textures characterize it. Just so, Barthes's "grain" concept can easily become a pretext for evading any real analysis of a singing voice, even on its own terms.

Allan Moore lists the traits he considers essential to analyzing a rock voice—range/register, resonance, attitude to pitch, and attitude to rhythm. The second of these is, in his opinion, "the best way to take into account" Barthes's "grain" concept. For Moore, resonance consists of vibrato, degrees of timbre, "placement" of the voice (nasal vs. chest cavities), and the implied physiological source of the tone (diaphragm or throat).[18] Yet, if the voice is really evincing implied identities, other factors such as vowel shaping, changes of dynamic, and modification of tone should also be important. Moore tends to neglect these and to disconnect vocal technique from the text being sung. One of the pleasures of considering the factors Moore does and does not mention is in seeing how they interact with texts to create odd, hybrid languages.

Besides, an offhand comment by a good listener often tells us more than a great deal of scholarly scrutiny. Country musician Charlie Hodge, for example, recalled of Presley that, "You [could] hear the different characters in his voice. He would be Billy Eckstine, he would be Bill Kenny of the Ink Spots, he would be Hank Snow—all these people became Elvis Presley by the time he started touring. He had all these people inside of him."[19] Hodge heard other voices interweaving in Presley's. And it was that complex entanglement of voices that gave Presley his "grain." Rock scholarship should pay closer attention to that aspect of vocalizing. Indeed, the "grain of the voice" as an analytical metaphor needs to be understood in connection with the "congregation of the voice"—my somewhat off-the-cuff term for the collection of personalities implied by a rock singer's delivery.[20]

The electric guitar also sings with its own "grain." Most scholarly books and articles concerning the guitar treat electric guitars as mere amplified versions of their progenitors. But the electric guitar has actually become a new pseudo-vocal instrument, one that differs from the "acoustic" (non-electric) guitar at least as much as the piano differed from the clavichord. Varying kinds of distortion define the new instrument's sound (calling into question the usefulness of a semantically loaded term like "distortion" in the first place). This is because rock guitarists discovered early on that the transformation of the "normal" sound of a guitar through electric or electronic means could dramatically intensify the expressive powers of the instrument. In other words, as Walser observes, "at a particular historical moment [electric guitar] distortion begins to be perceived in terms of power rather than failure, intentional transgression rather than accidental overload—as music rather than noise."[21]

The best sources on electric guitars are popular magazines like *Guitar, Guitar Player,* and *Guitar World.* These magazines contain interviews, articles, and advice columns, in which players discuss who influenced their idea of guitar sonority, whose "sound" they first wanted to emulate, and how they achieve their current sound. Meanwhile, the advertisements for various distortion devices demonstrate how powerfully the progeny of overdrive have permeated guitarists' tastes. Guitar distortion has grown into a huge family of closely related sounds. By tracing distortion from player to player and device to device, guitar magazines constitute a genealogical archive of fuzz.

While references to "garage" as a stylistic term appear increasingly in books and mainstream articles, the term initially gained ground in the liner notes to compilation albums and in published ephemera like "fanzines" (independently and inexpensively published tributes to specific artists or styles). In all sources, writers tend to dwell on one of three things—the bands' sociological significance, their musical competence, and their style of playing.

From a sociological perspective, some writers treat garage bands as a foil to the so-called British Invasion, in which British groups seemed to dominate the airwaves.[22] As one puts it:

> English critics like to speak of American rock since 1964 as a lame attempt to respond to the innovations of the Beatles and the English groups that have come since. Another typical example of cultural myopia.
>
> The truth is that the Beatles and their ilk were seen in the U.S. as a novel twist on the traditional rock and roll and contemporary soul that were already firmly established on American soil. And all the while, Americans were creating new musical trends so fast that the English never even started catching up.[23]

Another writer even proposes that Paul Revere and the Raiders were so named because they "helped repel a British Invasion in 1965."[24]

The chief problem with this nationalistic interpretation of garage bands is that some of the most celebrated garage bands transparently imitated the innovations of British groups, particularly those groups that offered themselves as stylistic alternatives to the Beatles. The garage bands covered hits by those groups (e.g., the Rolling Stones and the Yardbirds), borrowed riffs and vocal styles, and in some cases changed their names to make them sound British. Even Paul Revere and the Raiders borrowed much of the British Invasion style they were supposedly repelling. Their second album, ironically titled *Just Like Us!* includes covers of not only the Stones' "Satisfaction," but also the Animals' "I'm Crying," and Them's arrangement of "Baby, Please Don't Go."

Some writers define garage bands by their unfocused tastes and ama- teurish technique. One author claims that "what sets apart the best garage bands is the degree of intensity they achieved in copying or distorting the ideas of the trendsetting artists, the hipness of what they chose to inter- pret and how much of their own stamp they were able to put on it." This intensity, hipness, and distinctiveness supposedly grew from the bands' technical deficiency, what Don Waller calls the "practitioners' uncon- scious ineptitude."[25] Lester Bangs puts it bluntly: "The greatest garage bands could barely play."[26]

But when writers call a group a garage band, they often seem to mean that the band exemplified a new style, an early form of what is now known as "punk."[27] (Bangs calls it "protopunk.")[28] In describing the style, Bangs and other writers usually refer to the "distorted" vocals and electric gui- tar sounds. Garage rock is a style, as one author puts it, "characterized by snotty vocals, loud fuzz and distorted vocals and anti-social teen angst."[29] Beverly Paterson writes that garage singers "did little more than screech and squawk."[30] Dave Marsh identifies the "requirements of the genre" as "cheesy organ riffs [and] exaggerated lyric silliness."[31] Although this book attempts a deeper analysis of "garage" as a stylistic term, much more will undoubtedly be written in the coming years, as garage rock's importance to current styles looms larger.

By contrast, the idea of "psychedelic" music in the 1960s has already received much attention in popular magazines and some scholarly works. Edward Macan's *Rocking the Classics* discusses psychedelic music as a pre- cursor to progressive rock. In *Kaleidoscope Eyes: Psychedelic Rock from the '60s to the '90s,* Jim DeRogatis surveys the history of psychedelic music over four decades. Both books eschew real nuts-and-bolts analysis of what made music psychedelic. At the other end of the spectrum, Sheila Whiteley's *The Space Between the Notes: Rock and the Counter-Culture* downplays the history of psychedelia in favor of analysis—particularly analysis that tries to show how music can display "psychedelic coding." Whiteley suggests that the extended solos in the music (especially guitar solos) represent musical "trips." She also mentions six aspects of psychedelic music:

1. manipulation of timbres (blurred/bright/overlapping)
2. upward movement (connoting "psychedelic flight")
3. harmonies (oscillating/lurching)
4. rhythms (regular/irregular)
5. relationships (foreground/background)
6. collages[32]

Her ideas bear much in common with mine and both of us agree with the musicians who assert that hallucinogenic drugs inspired musical techniques.

But here is an area where one should not only put the music in historical context but also conduct careful interdisciplinary research. To understand a pharmaceutically derived music requires a good knowledge of pharmaceuticals. What I tried to demonstrate in the chapter on psychedelic music is how much one can learn about psychedelic music by reading the literature of psychedelic drugs. Admittedly, psychedelic music poses a unique case study—what other style of music is so explicitly linked to drugs?[33] But interdisciplinary study may well yield fruit in other rock categories. Consider, for example, how much one might learn about the style of Motown music by understanding auto manufacturing in Detroit, the structure of assembly lines, the techniques for modifying basic car designs, and even the quality of audio tone in automobile radio speakers.

The rock scholar, then, has many archives to consult: mainstream albums (whatever their format), cult albums (especially compilations), bootleg albums and tapes, rare rock records of almost every kind, popular magazines, fanzines, and, increasingly, the thousands of websites appearing on the internet—virtual fanzines. Only lastly should one consult scholarly journals and full-fledged books ("scholarly" or mass market-oriented). The diversity of this list often compels the student of rock to pursue an unorthodox line of research. The student can find many of rock's telling details only with a scavenging scholarship that relies somewhat on standard bibliographic guides and indices, but also browses fan magazines and thrift shops, trades tapes, and makes friends with collectors, the real archivists of the art of rock. And nowadays, the rock scholar must feel as comfortable with the hum of a computer as he or she once did with the hum of a microfilm viewer. The rock scholar must be as conversant with tape-trading as with note-taking. Only a thoroughgoing search of every source at hand will yield insights into rock's formidable sonic power and complexity.

Appendix 2: Names

From the 1950s through the 1960s popular bands changed the kinds of names they gave themselves. The change corresponded to the shift from "rock 'n' roll" to "rock"—the former more playful and high-spirited, the latter more "serious" and calculating. Rock names of the 1950s and early 1960s tended to exalt their owners into the high life, evoking images of sophistication and opulence. The names of the mid-1960s and beyond, however, tended to abase their owners not only into lower classes but even into lower life forms (e.g., animals). In the history of rock group names one can observe the passing of one form of desirable identity and the rise of another: the old ideals of suavity and charm mutated into new ideals of alienation and defiance.[1]

*

In the 1950s and early 1960s, hundreds of groups used names derived from musical terminology. Some simply borrowed the names of instruments (the Cellos, the Coronets, the Five Chimes, the Lyres). Many others used technical terms. They either invoked basic concepts of raw sound (the Vibes, the Vibranaires), adapted names from musical jargon (the Five Keys, the Sharps, the Chords, the Downbeats, the Largos), or, most commonly, attached the suffix "tones" to almost any other kind of term. Thus one encounters the Jaytones, the Youngtones, the Nobletones, the Quintones, the Gee Tones, the Mello-tones, the Val-tones, the Nu-tones, the

Guytones, the Tendertones, the Dreamtones, the Sharptones, the Harptones, the Velvetones, the Goldentones, and the Miracletones, to name only a few who made records during those years.

Hundreds of other groups derived names from the natural world, especially from phenomena of the sky and air. Some of these names referred to the course of the day (the Sunbeams, the Daylighters, the Moonbeams, the Moonlighters, the Moonglows, the Twilighters, the Midnighters), others to weather conditions (the Raindrops, the Rainbows). Many groups expanded the aerial concept into the realm of ornithology. Originally these bird names, chiefly associated with vocal harmony groups, may have been meant to connote songbirds: thus, the Swallows, the Robins, the Larks, the Bluejays, the Sparrows, the Nightingales (the Orioles, however, were named for the baseball team).[2] But since such species were rather quickly used up, many groups had to adopt the names of almost any sort of bird—the Parakeets, the Jayhawks, the Flamingos, the Quails, the Swans, the Pelicans, and even the Penguins.[3]

Although such musical and nature-based group names were common, most groups of this period tried to project a special kind of identity, one that was up-to-date, fashionable, upper-crust, and alluring. By connoting objects of high culture and titles of office, these group names conjured up an aristocratic air. They testified to the enduring power of the American dream, the drive for "upward mobility" that dominated the national character.

Reaching for a sense of sheer modernity, some groups tried to link themselves to "space-age" concerns. They took names that exploited the contemporary interest in exploration of the cosmos (the Meteors, the Rockets, the Rocketeers, the Radars, the Orbits) or names more generally alluding to technology, either in its general aspects (the Metallics, the Magnetics) or specific manifestations (the Neons, the Fluorescents). Perhaps the simplest way to project a "modern" identity was to borrow the name of a current automobile. Not only were cars common images of modernity, they were also a staple of teenage myth (e.g., "parking" as a sexual repast), and the literal vehicles for listening to broadcast music. Thus, we find such group names as the Chevelles, the El Dorados, the Cadillacs, the Fairlanes, the Bonnevilles, the Triumphs, the Colts, the Ramblers.

Pursuing an image of sophistication, groups used names that broadly suggested elements of high life (the Skyliners, the Terracetones, the Elegants, the Socialites, the Classics), or names that were more specific, appealing to the accoutrements of opulence—especially expensive fabrics and clothes (the Five Satins, the Velvets, the Cordovans, the Tuxedos, the Lapels, the Cuff Links) or flowers and jewelry (the Orchids, the Carnations, the Emeralds, the Pearls, the Four Gems, the Four Jewels). A few groups associated themselves with various sorts of mastery (the Superbs, the Highlights, the Limelites, the Premiers, the Masters, the Five Superiors, the Leaders), occasionally identifying themselves with some of the rewards of achievement (the Ovations, the Encores). Many tried to assert their desirability as male companions (the Bachelors, the Romeos, the Casanovas, the Playboys, the Consorts, the Romancers, the Enchanters, the Hearts, the Fascinations, the Passions), sometimes transforming adjectives into nominatives (the Debonairs, the Sentimentals, the Dappers, the Majestics). On one hand, groups proclaimed their alliance with the American educational system (the Academics, the Students, the Ivy Leaguers); on the other hand, they freely associated themselves with exotic internationalism (the Tangiers, the Moroccos, the Persians, the Turbans, the Sheiks). Ultimately, many groups placed themselves squarely in the realms of aristocracy: the Camelots, the Barons, the Counts, the Four Jacks, the Regents, the Esquires, the Pharaohs, the Love Lords, the Emperors, the Royals, the Royal Teens, and, of course, various sorts of kings (the Kings, the Mello Kings, the King Crooners, etc.).

In the early- to mid-1960s, while bird names tended to vanish, other 1950s-style names persisted. Specifically musical names appeared occasionally (the Beatmen, the Clefs, the Echoes, the Sonics, the Music Machine, the Modulation Corporation), and aristocratic allusions flourished (the Barons, the Squires, the Chancellors, Count and the Colony, the Counts, the Dukes, the Esquires, the Exchequers, the Fabulous Pharaohs, the Heralds, the Kingsmen, the Knights, the Noblemen, the Palace Guard, the Royal Guardsmen, and the Sires). Many groups turned these allusions into word plays (the Knights of Day, the Shadows of Knight, Last Knight, Count Five) or inside jokes (Sir Raleigh and the Coupons).[4] Other groups referred to aristocracy more obliquely (the Blue Scepter, the Chosen Few, the Continental V, the Country Gentlemen); some even connoted religious hierarchy (the Deacons). To enhance their aristocratic aura, a few used foreign languages: the Beaux Jens [*sic*], for example, who took their name from a French textbook belonging to a band member's girlfriend; they fancied themselves handsome young men, yet needed the European flair of the French phrase. A few groups from this period tried to show their sophistication by a kind of name-dropping, taking names derived from classics of literature, art, and music. Thus, one encounters the Age of Reason, the Bards, Beethoven's Fifth, the Brave New World, the Brothers Grim, the Epics, the Glass Menagerie, the Leaves of Grass, Oedipus and the Mothers, Peter and the Wolves, and many others.

In the mid-1960s group names changed dramatically. Beginning primarily with the British-based rhythm and blues bands, groups endeavored to distance themselves from their middle class origins, pursuing not the upper class but the lower. As George Melly put it, "The suburbs have thrown up most of the young people who are in conscious revolt. . . . Their only sin, and it's a minor one, is sometimes to lie about their origin. They pretend to be working class."[5] For some groups this was simply a matter of strategic marketing. Following Oldham's motto "For every star there is an anti-star," some groups probably chose a lower-class image in hopes of becoming the cultural complements of the slick groups that preceded them. Their names, of course, would need to denote that complementation.

Still another reason for these groups to feign working-class origins was to mythologize their quest for success: by exaggerating their essential lowliness, a successful group could more powerfully claim social achievement. Whereas the earlier rock group names tended to assert that one had already "made it," the new names emphasized that one was intent on making it against all odds. Mick Jagger put it well: "You have to remember that part of the hero image is making it from the bottom."[6] Many group names of the 1960s were no longer about having arrived, but about the struggle to get there—although it was not readily clear where "there" was.

The groups that emerged from the suburbs wanted to achieve a certain cultural authenticity, to show that they were in it not only for the money, but for art. Suburbia seemed an essentially inauthentic environment. The further from it one could go—in either direction—the more one acquired cultural legitimacy. And since the middle class from which most of these groups came had always been "rising" into the upper class, it seemed more genuine to aspire downward—to the "roots," one might say. By rejecting the trappings of their native social class, these groups achieved a kind of asceticism that was spiritually liberating. As Simon Frith wrote, "If rock is a way out of the working class, a path to riches, it is also a way out of the middle class, a path to bohemian freedoms."[7] For rock groups to fulfill what they considered their mission and calling, they needed names that freed them from their origins.

One can see the process at work in the naming of the Yardbirds. The group had begun as the Metropolis Blues Quartet—a simple, generic name that also connoted modern city life. When a fifth player joined, they decided that, rather than simply change to "quintet," they should look for a more suggestive name. The list of names they considered provides a good index of (sometimes contradictory) identities with which they thought to associate themselves: Roll Ups, Yardbirds, Dust, Hills, Memphis, River, Mud, Hobo, New, Old, Five, Backyard, Backwater, Dry, Motivators, River Water, Jailhouse, Camp, Town, City, Country, Leather, Wood, Goodtime, Thames, Island, Evening. "Yardbirds" finally won out, because of lead singer Keith Relf's association of the word "yardbird" with the transient bohemian life described in the works of Jack Kerouac.[8]

It was the sort of name (and corresponding image) that had only been touched upon in the 1950s and early 1960s (the Tramps, the Wanderers, and the Drifters—although the latter supposedly referred to the group members having "drifted" among other bands).[9] But it was just the sort of name that circulated widely in the mid-1960s. Indeed, groups began to take names that not only suggested commonness, transience, or alienation, but also criminality, primitivism, even bestiality—a kind of devolutionary chain of identities with which groups seemed eager to link themselves.

Rejecting the self-asserting aristocratic names so popular in the 1950s, groups chose nondescript or self-effacing names: the Familiars, the Souls, the Faces in the Crowd, the Mortals, We the People, Those Guys, Those Boys, or simply, Them. Some groups moved beyond the implicit anonymity of such names to names openly suggesting some sort of estrangement: the Abandoned, the Down and Out, the Down Children, the Nomads, the Exiles, the Four Strangers, the Heathens, the Immigrants, the Outsiders, the Outcasts, the Slaves, the Kings of Oblivion. Some groups projected an air of alienation through names connoting the American western frontier: the Hunters, the Huntsmen, Beaver and the Trappers, the Chapparals, the Bounty Hunters, and, with a characteristic word play, the Raunch Hands. Such names implied ruggedness and self-reliance.

Many groups tried to break cultural taboos about violence, aggression, primitivism, and sexuality. The Kinks, for example, began as the Ravens— one of the common bird names of 1950s groups. But this name failed to satisfy the growing need for unconventionality. So in 1964 the Ravens became the Kinks in order to suggest "kinkyness"—"something newsy, naughty," Ray Davies explained, "but just on the borderline of acceptability." (To illustrate the name the group even had pictures taken of themselves with whips, chains, and leather garb.)[10] Other groups followed the same impulse, identifying themselves with the alienation of transgressors:

the Bad Boys, the Bad Seeds, the Bad Habits, the Bandits, the Rogues, the Fugitives, the Inmates, the Outlaws, the Renegades, the Rogues, the Scoundrels, the Charlatans, the Dirty Shames, the Caretakers of Deception, and Corruption, Inc. While those names suggested common human flaws, another class of names suggested deeper transgressions, identifying their wearers as enemies to God (the Children of Darkness, the Original Sinners, Satan and the D-Men, the Satans, Satan's Breed, the Evil, the Evil I, the Fallen Angels, the Lost Souls). A few groups simply identified themselves with death (the Graveyard Five, the Macabre, the Headstones, the Tombstones, and the Undertakers).

It was only a step from such names to outright aggressive ones. Groups virtually assaulted their audience with new forms of hostile, even threatening monikers: the Attack, the Avengers, the Invaders, the Raiders, the Executioners, the Intruders, the Hangmen, the Vandals, the Plagues, and the Bohemian Vendetta. A few other groups used names based on weaponry and deadly machinery: the Gun, Jagged Edge, the Buzzsaw, and, perhaps the most inventive, the Guilloteens.

Groups also gave themselves names suggesting forms of mental illness (the Hysterics, the Psychopaths, the Raving Mad, the Panicks). Similarly, they took names that bespoke a retreat into the private world of drug-induced dreams and hallucinations, as well as a defiance of the prevailing laws (the Visions, the Velvet Illusions, the Beautiful Daze, Euphoria, Euphoria's Id). And related names linked their owners to the mental and social alienation found in mysticism and the occult (the Infinite Pyramid, the Infinite Staircase, the Mystic Tide, the Mystic Crystal Astrologic Band).

But perhaps the most common "downwardly mobile" names identified the groups as pre-civilized: the Cavemen, the Primitives, the Hairy Ones, the Woolies, the Wooly Ones, the Untamed, the Pack, the Bushmen, the Cavedwellers, the Barbarians, the Young Savages, and the Wild Things—this last taken from the hit by the Troggs, a name that itself was short for "troglodytes." Many groups, like the Animals, extended this principle down the evolutionary ladder, even delineating various sub-human species: reptiles (the Cobras, the Iguanas), mammals (the Primates, the Skunks, the Swamp Rats, the Foul Dogs), insects (the Flies, the Termites, the Bugs, King Beez, the Spyders), or sea creatures (the Crabs, the Barracudas)—but almost never birds (except, of course, the Byrds). Beneath these species, many names referred to plant life (the Leaves, the Seeds, the Weeds, the Vejtables, the Giant Sunflower), the soil (the Grains of Sand, the Pebbles), or even the primordial (the Dirty Filthy Mud). Many of the names alluding to plant life derived from their proprietors' interest in the natural sources of psychedelics (Children of the Mushroom, the Magic Mushrooms, the Herbal Mixture). But in some cases, it must be conceded, purely practical concerns influenced the names. Sky Saxon recalls the origins of his group's name the Seeds: "I had a band called the Vikings which had a down-to earth sound. . . . Since we couldn't afford Viking costumes we changed our name to the Seeds [representing] growth, plants and vegetables, and making people conscious to get back to the earth. It was also easy to dress since we could dress like farmers if we wanted."[11]

As we have seen, many group names included word play or deliberate misspelling. Only occasionally did such devices appear in earlier years (e.g., the Rip-Chords, the C-Quinns). But they abounded in the mid-1960s. The Beatles provided the principal model here, taking the name of the Crickets (Buddy Holly's band), changing the species, then modifying the spelling so as to play on the word "beat." Other groups followed suit, so much so that common traits emerged, almost as though they were the components of a new phonetics:

Certain consonants were routinely transformed: a hard "s" became a "c" (the Ceeds), a soft "s" became a "z" (the Boyz, the Treez, the Human Beinz), and a hard "ch" became simply a hard "c" (the Cicadelics). In the last example we can also see one of the more common vowel-transforming devices at work, the substitution of an "i" for a "y" (or vice versa). The Byrds provide the best known example; their drummer recalls that the change "gave [the name] a bit of flair."[12] Others groups did likewise: the Chaynes, the Chylds, the Chymes, Cirkyt, Crome Syrcus, the Cyrkle, and Cykle, to name a few (meanwhile, the Turtles was originally supposed to be the "Tyrtles").[13] To use "ea" for "e" or "ee" was also common (the Weads, the Heard—the latter also a word play). Various other transformations occasionally appeared, among consonants (the Stumbling Blox, the Bear Fax, the Vejtables) and vowels (the Groop, the Gruve, the City Zu, the Dirty Wurds). Final consonants were doubled (the Endd, the Badd Boys), or an "e" added, perhaps to give a European flair (the Herde). And words sometimes were split into components, creating further word plays (the D-Coys, the In-Sect).

Variant spellings had several functions. On a superficial level, they expressed a certain banal cleverness. They also bespoke musicality by subverting normal written spelling to the pure sounds of the words. Perhaps most important, variant spellings evoked primitivism. Their authors feigned poor education through a childlike sort of illiteracy. Deliberate misspelling reinforced the sense of downward mobility that so many of the names connoted in the first place.

The playful distortion of phonemes led to distortion at the syntactic level—flamboyant names consisting of a noun prefixed by an adjective that didn't fit it. Some simply modified animal names (the Neurotic Sheep, the Barking Spyders, Bubble Puppy, Iron Butterfly).[14] The most common, however, joined odd modifiers to foods (the Electric Prunes, the Blue Banana, Moby Grape)[15] or linked flavor names to non-edible items (the Chocolate Watchband, the Chocolate Balloon, the Chocolate Tunnel, the Chocolate Pickles, the Strawberry Alarm Clock, the Marshmallow Steamshovel, the Lemon Fog).[16]

These surrealistic names suggested the alienation of drug use: they were psychedelic, making the strange associations of the dreaming (or LSD-saturated) mind. They also rejected the old dualisms of old/new, rich/poor, establishment/bohemian, and simply retreated into the pure unconscious, the source of art. The collision of ideas provoked by these names required the observer to bridge the syntactic gap, relinquishing logic in favor of intuition. As Dave Laing put it, "Each word in the phrase came from outside the paradigm of words which could 'meaningfully' connect with the other. . . . This meaninglessness then effectively becomes the significance of the term itself in a rock music context: it is signalled that this name, and through analogy this band, is against the established order of meaning, is in some way avant-garde."[17] Poggioli himself identifies this trait: an avant garde shows itself partly in the "deliberate use of an idiom all its own, a quasi-private jargon. . . . the desire of a group of youths to distinguish themselves by a kind of secret language . . . [a] linguistic hermeticism."[18]

Many groups tried to make the origins of their names seem almost accidental. The bands' bohemian pretenses dictated that a name not seem labored. It should be a spontaneous expression of an attitude, a sudden imprint of the group's collective unconscious. This principle is well demonstrated in the liner notes to the Leaves' first album, which expressed their pride in the name's casual inception: "The whole thing began on a windy California afternoon as the boys sat in a backyard under swaying Eucalyptus and Sycamore. They had all been quiet for a time until, to break the silence, someone asked 'What's happening?' Glancing at the leaves cascading down from the trees, Ambrose Ray replied in his jovially sarcastic manner, 'The leaves are happening.' And those few words brought about the naming and launching of a new popular music group."[19] Buffalo Springfield took its name from a steamroller they observed paving the streets outside the house where they rehearsed: on its side were the two city names "Buffalo, Springfield."[20] The Grateful Dead took its name by one member of the group randomly stabbing his finger in the dictionary.[21] Even groups who chose their names more deliberately thought it useless to give the name any afterthought. As Chris Dreja of the Yardbirds said, "Once the name was decided, we never gave it a second thought; it was perfect. That's the way it has to be—people who sit around fretting over whether they've made the right choice of name to represent anything have got problems."[22]

But whether by design or serendipity, rock groups intended their names to upturn the old cultural aspirations, undo conventions of language, and even discard historical categories of reason. This allowed them to symbolically reclaim the institution of music from the cultural elite and reinvent it as the common man's possession. Much is made of the literature of rock, and many commentators dwell on the lyrics of songs as the principal resource for that literature. But group names must remain the proto-literature of the art, the most elemental poetic expressions of rock.

Notes

Preface

1. For a discussion of the diversity of definitions of rock, see Allan F. Moore, *Rock, the Primary Text: Developing a Musicology of Rock* (Buckingham, England: Open University Press, 1993), 3–4; and Theodore Gracyk, *Rhythm and Noise: An Aesthetics of Rock* (Durham, N.C.: Duke University Press, 1996), 2–6.

2. Charles Hamm, *Music in the New World* (New York: Norton, 1982), 646–47.

3. Quoted in Gracyk, *Rhythm and Noise,* 9. For a fine summary of the Beatles' and Dylan's combined influences see Robert Palmer, *Rock & Roll: An Unruly History* (New York: Harmony Books, 1995), 99–111.

4. Scholarly authors often ask the question, only to retreat from answering it. See, for example, Peter Wicke, *Rock Music: Culture, Aesthetics and Sociology,* trans. Rachel Fogg (Cambridge: Cambridge University Press, 1990), 1–3.

5. Richard Middleton, *Studying Popular Music* (Milton Keynes, England: Open University Press, 1990), 112.

Chapter 1: The Against-the-Grain of the Voice

1. Jagger interviewed by Jonathan Cott, in Peter Herbst, ed., *The Rolling Stone Interviews, 1967–1980: Talking with the Legends of Rock & Roll* (New York: St. Martins/Rolling Stone Press, 1981), 49.

2. Bruce Cook, "Jagger and the Stones," *Commonweal* 102 (20 June 1975): 212.

3. The three quotes are from A. E. Hotchner, *Blown Away* (New York: Simon and Schuster, 1990), 116, 81, and 73, respectively.

4. See my remarks on the popularity of this term in appendix 1.

5. I take this idea from a remark by Robert Christgau, *Any Old Way You Choose It: Rock and Other Pop Music, 1967–1973* (Baltimore: Penguin, 1973), 222: "Like so many extraordinary voices, Jagger's defied description by contradicting itself."

6. Simon Frith, *Music for Pleasure* (Cambridge: Polity Press, 1988), 120.

7. I focus entirely on *male* voices, for all the reasons discussed by Moore, *Rock, the Primary Text,* 41.

8. The African-American way of distorting the voice for effect is sometimes described in relation to the aesthetic of "expression" with the voice. See Wicke, *Rock Music,* 19.

9. One can trace this vocal device to the microphone technique of a very different singer, the pop vocalist Bing Crosby. Understanding how the microphone could not only project "normal" singing but also convey the subtleties of a closely placed voice, Crosby developed a peculiar "conversational intimacy" with the mike. The roar of rhythm and blues singers derived from an era before the use of the microphone as a reinforcing device. Holly's technique arose in an era that took the microphone for granted, particularly as Crosby had used it. See Robert Christgau, "The Prehistory of Rock 'n' Roll," *Details* 11 (July 1992): 69.

10. I borrow the term "baby talk" from Jonathan Cott, "Buddy Holly," in Jim Miller, ed., *The Rolling Stone Illustrated History of Rock & Roll,* rev. 2d ed. (New York: Random House/Rolling Stone Press, 1980), 78. While baby talk seems a typically white technique, it can be heard in Chuck Berry's "No Particular Place to Go" (the lines "So I told her softly and sincere / and she leaned and whispered in my ear").

11. It is hard to say, but this may be the quality of Lindsay's vocalizing that leads Richard Meltzer to consider the Raiders an "anti-tongue" group, by which he means that "there's slick tension as to how that which [in the vocal] will actually be resolved," given all of the "overly obvious tongue indicators" that are projected in the music. See R. Meltzer, *The Aesthetics of Rock* (New York: Something Else Press, 1970), 131.

12. Quoted in Christgau, *Any Old Way You Choose It,* 224.

13. From a 1973 interview with Tony Scaduto, reprinted in David Dalton, ed., *The Rolling Stones: The First Twenty Years* (London: Thames and Hudson, 1981), 18.

14. Quoted in Tom Russell and Sylvia Tyson, eds., *And Then I Wrote: The Songwriter Speaks* (Vancouver: Arsenal Pulp Press, 1995), 80.

15. Dalton, *Rolling Stones,* 36

16. Herbst, *Rolling Stone Interviews,* 49.

17. Dalton, *Rolling Stones,* 32

18. The care that Jagger takes with his voice accounts for assessments such as this: "Mick has enormous stamina. He can go on singing for hours and hours nonstop—and always turning in a great performance" (Bobby Abrams, "What Motherfuckin' Heavies," in Jonathan Eisen, ed., *The Age of Rock 2: Sights and Sounds of the American Cultural Revolution* [New York: Vintage, 1970], 46). According to Sally Arnold, when doctors wanted to remove Jagger's tonsils, "Mick was terrified that it would change his voice so he wouldn't let them do it" (quoted in Hotchner, *Blown Away,* 211). Jagger explained that "you've got to take care of your voice," including getting plenty of rest, avoiding drugs, and gargling with glycerine three times a day—see *Mick Jagger in His Own Words,* comp. "Miles" (New York: Delilah/ Putnam, 1982), 72.

19. Jagger may have adapted this technique from the singing of bluesman Slim Harpo, who characteristically sang in a flat, nearly emotionless voice.

20. The quote is from Christgau, *Any Old Way You Choose It,* 224.

21. According to one observer, Jagger even affected his own cockney accent. Michael Prowdlock says that "Mick Jagger can speak perfectly acceptable English, but he chooses to speak with a Cockney accent he invented" (in Hotchner, *Blown Away,* 49).

22. Examples of these include the King's Ransom ("Shame"), the Sinners ("Nice Try"), the Bougalieu ("Let's Do Wrong"), the Magic Plants ("I'm a Nothin'"), the Avengers ("Be a Cave Man"), the Vejtables ("Feel the Music"), the Grains of Sand ("Goin' Away Baby"), the Rovin' Flames ("How Many Times"), the Chocolate Watchband ("Are You Gonna Be There [At the Love-In]?"), and the Remains ("Say You're Sorry"), to name only a few more transparent instances of Jagger-imitating.

23. Lester Bangs, "Protopunk: The Garage Bands," in Miller, *Rolling Stone Illustrated History,* 263, refers to Saxon's "Mick Jagger routine"; Harold Bronson, Notes to *Nuggets, Volume Two: Punk* (Rhino: RNLP 026), writes that Saxon "fashioned himself as an American Jagger."

24. In Dave Marsh and John Swenson, eds., *The New Rolling Stone Record Guide* (New York: Random House/Rolling Stone Press, 1983), 452. Saxon's persona has not helped his reception. He seems to some a slightly burned-out remnant of psychedelia. Don Waller, Notes to *Nuggets, Volume One: The Hits* (Rhino RNLP 025), assesses him curtly: "if Nancy Reagan *really* wanted to keep schoolkids off dope, she'd show 'em a filmed conversation with what's left of Sky Saxon." Nevertheless, Saxon touts his role in rock history—consider the 1987 interview with him in Allan Vorda, *Psychedelic Psounds: Interviews from A to Z with 60s Psychedelic and Garage Bands* (N.p.: Borderline Productions, 1994), 173–78.

25. Not only in the hit "Pushin' Too Hard" (1966), but in the extremely similar tracks on the group's first album, "Evil Hoodoo," "Try to Understand," and "You Can't Be Trusted."

26. Especially on the word "me" at the end of each chorus

27. See the Music Machine compact disc review by Gordon Spencer in *Discoveries* 99 (August 1996): 44.

28. Notes to Julie London, *Lonely Girl* (Liberty LRP 3012).

Chapter 2: The Fuzz

1. Quoted in "Distortion Tips from the Loud & Mighty," *Guitar Player* 26 (October 1992): 45.

2. See, for example, the Ellington Band's 1927 recording of "East St. Louis Toodle-oo." My thanks to Brian Harker for providing me with recordings of this phenomenon. See also Barry Kernfeld, ed., *The New Grove Dictionary of Jazz* (New York, Macmillan, 1988), s.v. "Growl."

3. Examples abound: some of the best are the buzzing baritone sax opening of Chuck Higgins's "Pachuko Hop" (1953), the playing of Joe Tillman in Lloyd Lambert's "Whistlin' Joe" (1955), and the two-note saxophone bass line in Little Anthony and the Imperials "I'm Alright" (1958).

4. Humphrey Lyttelton, *New Musical Express,* quoted in Charlie Gillett, *The Sound of the City: The Rise of Rock and Roll,* rev. 2d ed. (New York: Pantheon, 1983), 258.

5. Quoted in Karen Schoemer, "Screamin' Jay Hawkins as Pitchman and Actor," *New York Times,* 5 April 1991, sec. C, 15.

6. The overdriving of the amplifier created, in effect, a band-pass filter that clipped the original signal's wave-form into something close to a square wave, full of high-amplitude overtones.

7. Robert Palmer, "The Church of the Sonic Guitar," *Southern Atlantic Quarterly* 90 (Fall 1991): 656.

8. See John Broven, *Rhythm and Blues in New Orleans* (Gretna, La.: Pelican, 1988), 54.

9. See the discussions of Slim's high-volume technique in Jas Obrecht, ed., *Blues Guitar: The Men Who Made the Music* (San Francisco: GPI Books, 1990), 134; also Palmer, "Church of the Sonic Guitar," 663–66.

10. John Platt et al., *Yardbirds* (London: Sidgwick and Jackson, 1983), 23.

11. Quoted in Palmer, *Rock & Roll,* 115.

12. Elizabeth Kaye, "The Rolling Stone Interview: Sam Phillips," *Rolling Stone* 467 (13 February 1986): 85.

13. Sam Phillips, quoted in Robert Palmer, *Deep Blues* (New York: Viking, 1981), 222.

14. For this and other background to the recording, see Jim Dawson and Steve Propes, *What Was the First Rock'n'Roll Record?* (Boston: Faber, 1992), 88–91.

15. Burlison quoted in Dan Forte, "The Pioneers of Rock Guitar," *Musician, Player & Listener* 43 (May 1982): 33.

16. Quoted in Forte, "Pioneers of Rock Guitar," 33.

17. This quote and the following one are from Mark Ribowsky, *He's a Rebel* (New York: Dutton, 1989), 126–27.

18. According to Duane Eddy, Phil Everly actually came up with the title after producer Archie Bleyer played him the finished recording. See Wayne Jancik, "The Definitive Duane Eddy Interview," *Discoveries* 71 (April 1994): 21.

19. At the third cycle of the blues progression, however, Wray introduces a rapid-strummed tremolo. When it ceases, the *electronic* tremolo gradually takes over.

20. Quoted in Notes to *Here Are the Ultimate Sonics* (Etiquette ETCD 024027).

21. Jas Obrecht, "Effects on Records: Pioneers and Prime Movers," *Guitar Player* 17 (June 1983): 26–28.

22. Jon Savage, *The Kinks: The Official Biography* (London: Faber, 1984), 32.

23. My dating of this device comes from telephone conversations with Walter Carter and J. T. Riboloff (both at Gibson Incorporated), 7 August 1995, and the comments of Roger Mayer in John Seabury and Charles Shaar Murray, "In Search of Volume: Guitar Amplification in the '60s," in Paul Trynka, ed., *The Electric Guitar: An Illustrated History* (San Francisco: Chronicle Books, 1995): 85.

24. The information in this paragraph comes primarily from Jas Obrecht and Bruce Bergman, "Roger Mayer: Electronics Wizard," *Guitar Player* 13 (February 1979): 47.

25. See Platt et al., *Yardbirds,* 55. Both versions may be heard on several compilations, e.g., *The Yardbirds: The Studio Sessions, 1964–1967* (Charly Records CD 187).

26. Quoted in Dalton, *Rolling Stones,* 53.

27. His comment about it being a "gimmick" may be found in Victor Bockris, *Keith Richards: The Biography* (New York: Poseidon, 1993), 93.

28. This and all the Richards quotes in this paragraph are taken from Dalton, *Rolling Stones,* 53.

29. The show was *Green Acres,* which premiered September 1965. The guitar was played by Tommy Tedesco, who used a Maestro pedal.

30. Craig Anderton, "Build a 'Fuzzbox' for Under $3," *Popular Electronics* 26 (January 1967): 87–92.

31. Mitch Mitchell with John Platt, *Jimi Hendrix: Inside the Experience* (New York: St. Martin's, 1990), 43.

32. Eric Barrett, "A Roadie's Nightmare," *Guitar Player* 9 (September 1975): 33.

33. Palmer, "Church of the Sonic Guitar," 651.

34. Quoted in "Distortion Tips," 45.

35. Quoted in ibid., 47.

36. Quoted in Notes to *Here Are the Ultimate Sonics.*

37. Quoted in Chris Gill, "Dialing for Distortion: Sound Advice from 10 Top Producers," *Guitar Player* 26 (October 1992): 86.

38. Kim Thayl, quoted in "Distortion Tips," 46.

39. The term "buzzsaw" comes from the fuzztone record of that title by the Gee Cees (led by Glen Campbell), issued ca. 1962.

40. Unattributed quote in Obrecht, *Blues Guitar,* 134.

Chapter 3: Avant Garage

1. A sampling: the generic liner notes on the back of CDs in the *Pebbles* series (ESD Digital) refer to "the brave and demented garage rock heroes of the fabulous sixties"; Peter Blecha, Notes to *Nuggets; Volume Eight: The Northwest* (Rhino Records RNLP 70032) refers to the recordings on that album as "mid-'60's garage-rock, seminal proto-punk"; the unsigned review of Elektra Records' *Nuggets: Original Artyfacts from the First Psychedelic Era, 1965–1968* (in *Rolling Stone,* 27 August 1987) quotes Jeff Conolly referring to this record as "the granddaddy of the garage-rock movement"; Jon Pareles and Patricia Romanokski, eds., *The Rolling Stone Encyclopedia of Rock & Roll* (New York: Rolling Stone/Summit, 1983), 494, refers to "the early-to-mid-Sixties garage-rock boom."

2. Both of these terms appear in early 1990s record lists from Bomp! Records (Burbank, California).

3. Julie Burchill and Tony Parsons, *The Boy Looked at Johnny: The Obituary of Rock and Roll* (London: Pluto Press, 1978), 2.

4. Charlie Gillett, *The Sound of the City: The Rise of Rock and Roll,* rev. ed. (New York: Pantheon, 1983), 313–14.

5. Burchill and Parsons, *Boy Looked at Johnny,* 1. Don Waller (in his notes to *Nuggets; Volume One: The Hits,* Rhino RNLP 025) humorously describes a typical garage band in pre- and post–British Invasion incarnations. The members of such a band consisted of "one kid who'd grown up copying Chet Atkins licks on his uncle's hollow-body [guitar], another who'd had ten years of classical piano lessons, a hyperactive woodshop dropout on drums, a lead singer with a range of three-and-a half notes and a bass player brought in for his ability to attract girls." After borrowing money for instruments and rehearsing in a garage, "their first paying gigs came in '63 or '64 when they called themselves, say, Thee Royal Coachmen and

rocked out with raunchy instrumentals and R&B standards. . . . After a year of play-
ing for junior high school dances, they'd updated their repertoire to include . . . the
Rolling Stones . . . and the entire first side of *Having a Rave-Up with the Yardbirds*. . . .
Now calling themselves, oh, the Savage Cabbage, [they] won a nearby Kustom Kar
Show's Battle of the Bands with their crowd-pleasing six-minute workout on Van
Morrison's seminal 'Gloria.' . . . The Grand Prize was a record contract awarded by
the boys' new manager: a local DJ, who put them in the nearest cheapest studio
with a dinosaur for an engineer."

6. Wayne Wadhams, quoted in Joseph Tortelli, "Underrated, Largely Forgotten:
The D-Men/Fifth Estate," *Discoveries* 64 (September 1993): 36.

7. Mark Volman, quoted in John Wooley, "Mark Volman: The Battles and the
Bands," *Discoveries* 106 (March 1997): 42.

8. Mark Volman, quoted in Wooley, "Mark Volman," 42.

9. Even if a group did not win a battle of the bands, however, it could still (if it
had the money) produce its own record, since several major record manufacturers would hire themselves out for even small runs of independent records—see
Aram Heller, *Till the Stroke of Dawn: A Discography of New England Garage Bands from
the 1960s* (Newtonville, Mass.: Stanton Park Records, 1993), [iii].

10. Ken Forssi, in Peter Kurtz, "Revelations: An interview with Ken Forssi of
Love," *Discoveries* 93 (February 1996): 36. The quotation from Dalley comes from
a telephone conversation with the author, 3 April 1997.

11. Dalton, *Rolling Stones,* 18.

12. Renato Poggioli, *The Theory of the Avant-Garde,* trans. Gerald Fitzgerald (Cambridge: Harvard University Press, 1968), 25.

13. The quotes are from Poggioli, *Theory of the Avant Garde,* 29, and F. J. Marinetti, "Down with the Tango and Parsifal!" reprinted in Nicolas Slonimsky, *Music since
1900,* 4th ed. (New York: Scribner's, 1971), 1302–3. The topic of masculinism in
modern art is treated in Catherine Parsons Smith, "'A Distinguishing Virility': Fem-
inism and Modernism in American Art Music," in Susan C. Cook and Judy S. Tsou,
eds., *Cecilia Reclaimed: Feminist Perspectives on Gender and Music* (Urbana: University of Illinois Press, 1994), 90–106. We should add that the machismo one sees in
the deportment of garage bands is often the machismo of masochism: even if the
players were working to the limit of their technique the result often sounded like
self-constraint and narrow routines; the singing often sounded like self-abuse, the
musical equivalent of tight collars. In that respect it resembled the fascist aesthetic to which futurism adapted so well. As Susan Sontag puts it, "Fascist aesthetics is
based on the containment of vital forces; movements are confined, held tight, held
in." *Under the Sign of Saturn* (New York: Farrar, Straus, Giroux, 1980), 93.

14. Poggioli, *Theory of the Avant-Garde,* 30–31.

15. "If the avant-garde has an etiquette," Poggioli suggests, "it consists of pervert-
ing and wholly subverting conventional deportment" (*Theory of the Avant-Garde,*
31).

16. This is the characterization of Dalton, *Rolling Stones,* 34.

17. See Jonathan D. Kramer, *The Time of Music: New Meanings, New Temporalities,
New Listening Strategies* (New York: Schirmer, 1988), 97. Allan Moore discusses the
problem of defining "beat" with respect to rock in *Rock, the Primary Text,* 32.

18. Quoted in Dave Laing, *One Chord Wonders: Power and Meaning in Punk Rock* (Milton Keynes, England: Open University Press, 1985), 61. In more technical terms, the backbeat superimposes an iambic meter on a trochaic meter, the former defined by dynamic and timbral stresses in the rhythm section—e.g., an accented snare drum attack—and the latter defined by the bass drum and rhythmic groupings in the vocal melody.

To articulate the backbeat, a drummer would usually play, as a minimum, a bass drum attack on beats one and three; a snare drum attack on beats two and four; and a continuous series of light attacks on the "ride" cymbal. "Fills," improvised ideas involving tom-tom, snare, and crash cymbal, appeared generally between phrases or sub-phrases and virtually always at the end of sections (verse, bridge, etc.).

19. The backbeat also maps onto a single measure a larger pattern of emphasis in rock 'n' roll, since there the second and fourth of every group of four measures typically carry greater dynamic and semantic weight than the first and third. Of course, there is some debate about the definition of accent in these larger, so-called hypermetrical structures. See the summary in Kramer, *Time of Music*, 84–96. (I am favoring the Arthur Komar point of view for understanding rock's hypermetrical accentuation.)

20. Grosvenor W. Cooper and Leonard B. Meyer, *The Rhythmic Structure of Music* (Chicago: University of Chicago, 1960), 3.

21. This is an idea at least as old as the Renaissance notion of "tactus." For a recent note on heartbeat and musical rhythm, see H. P. Koepchen et al., "Physiological Rhythmicity and Music in Medicine," in Ralph Spingte and Roland Droh, eds., *Music Medicine* (St. Louis: MMB Music, 1992), 39–41.

22. All of this sort of ambiguity—most obviously in Bo Diddley's case—is ultimately traceable to the layering of pulses and tempi in African and African-derived music (i.e., in the Caribbean isles, South America, etc.). For my purposes here, however, I am limiting the discussion to those rock-related styles that directly affected one another through recordings and broadcasting.

23. In jazz, the practice is sometimes called "double-time feel."

24. This was usually a one- or two-chord ostinato (a "vamp," often oscillating between I and vi, one measure apiece), while a short phrase of text (e.g., "He's alright") is repeated responsorially. In an actual service, particularly late at night, a coda might last for fifteen minutes or more, perhaps subtly transforming along the way, and serving as the accompaniment to spontaneous, improvised "dancing in the Spirit."

25. Laing, *One Chord Wonders*, 61. See Allan Moore's critique of the monad concept in *Rock, the Primary Text*, 113.

26. Deryck Cooke, *The Language of Music* (Oxford: Oxford University Press, 1959), 98.

27. Although this recording has no snare drum, the close-miked tambourine on every beat gives the song the appearance of having no metric accentuation.

28. Indeed, for some observers, the rhythmic monad became the most distinctive aspect of Motown style—see Jon Landau, "A Whiter Shade of Black," in Jonathan Eisen, ed., *The Age of Rock: Sounds of the American Cultural Revolution* (New York: Random House, 1969), 300–301.

29. Cooke, *Language of Music*, 99.

30. Dave Marsh, *The Heart of Rock & Soul: The 1001 Greatest Singles Ever Made* (New York: New American Library, 1989), 226.

31. This is the hit studio version; their live version (on *Five Live* and the American album *Having a Rave-Up with the Yardbirds*) is actually somewhat slower (a solid ♩ = 138).

32. Cf. Elvis Presley's use of vastly accelerated tempos in his covers of "Good Rockin' Tonight" (1954) and "Mystery Train" (1955).

33. Dalton, *Rolling Stones*, 33–35.

34. Platt et al., *Yardbirds*, 37.

35. The W. C. Fields Memorial Electric String Band does similarly in their original version of "I'm Not Your Stepping Stone," later a hit not only for the Raiders but also for the Monkees (and a major influence on later British punk groups such as the Sex Pistols).

36. See, for corroborating examples, songs like the Colony's "All I Want," the Answer's "I'll Be In" (1965), the Lyrics' "They Can't Hurt Me," the Odds and Ends' "Cause You Don't Love Me" (1966), and the Dirty Shames' "I Don't Care" (1966). In these songs the rhythmic monad connoted both a primal sense of authority and a transcendent indifference.

37. The title comes from the song of that name by the Adverts.

38. Notes to *Pebbles*, vol. 4 [CD] (East Side Digital, ESD 80362).

39. Notes to *Here Are the Ultimate Sonics*.

40. Laing, *One Chord Wonders*, 60.

41. Sonny Boy Williamson's "Help Me" (1963), a favorite among British rhythm-and-blues oriented groups, copied the same riff from the MGs' recording.

42. Indeed the ♭VII chord was rare in the more popular forms of rock, such as doowop. Frank Zappa recalls, "Very seldom would you . . . hear someone going from I to flat VII. There were only a few examples of *that* type of harmonic deviation during the fifties . . . so our chord progressions were not exactly part of that tradition" (Frank Zappa with Peter Occhiogrosso, *The Real Frank Zappa Book* [New York: Poseidon, 1989], 88–89). Zappa cites the Bel-Aires' "This Paradise" as "the best" example of I-♭VII motion in the doo-wop tradition.

43. The Seeds use a minor tonic chord. Many garage bands use this simple oscillating harmonic pattern (with either a major or a minor tonic) in the verses and choruses of their songs only, and provide some sort of bridge for contrast and reorientation of the listener.

44. In some the basic progression of I-♭III-IV moves directly to the dominant, which prepares for the return of I, yielding a four-chord ostinato thus: I-♭III | IV-V. This more aggressive, upward-driving progression often accompanies more aggressive texts. Thus, the ostinato of the Avengers' "Be a Cave Man" (chorus: "be a cave man, keep her in line") or the Wooly Ones' "Put Her Down" (text: "put her down and act like a man").

45. The Kingsmen's version of "Louie Louie," however, features a *minor* dominant, avoiding the leading tone in favor of the flatted seventh scale degree so endemic to the blues. Their variation yields a distinctively colored progression (I-

IV | *v*-IV) that has been quite explicitly copied (even in voicing and timbres) by the Remains in "Why Do I Cry?" (1967).

46. In that light some groups applied wave motion to the "Gloria" complex: the Grains of Sand, for example, in "That's Where Happiness Began," expand the "Louie Louie" progression into I-IV | ♭VII-IV.

47. Groups often used the progression in "new" songs: see not only the overt revision of "Gloria" by the Belles (retitled "Melvin"), but also the Silver Fleet's "Look Out World," Kempy and the Guardians' "Love for a Price" (verse only), and the Brymers' "Sacrifice," in which the double-plagal motion is attached to each two measures of tonic in the original progression, thus: I | ♭VII-IV.

48. In rhythm and blues and rock 'n' roll, one-measure *non-transposable* riffs appear seldom—but they do appear, usually as bass-oriented ideas playing on a cell composed of scale degrees 1, ♭3, and 4, and its transposition at the dominant level (5, ♭7, 8). (These two together comprise a minor pentatonic scale.) In both cases, the riff tends to end on the tonic note. (Muddy Waters' riff to "Hoochie Coochie Man" and Bo Diddley's riff to "I'm a Man" are standard, the former approaching the tonic from the dominant below [+3, +2 half-steps], the latter from the subdominant above [−2, −3].) One-measure transposable riffs, on the other hand, tended to be simple arpeggiations of the primary triads. These appeared frequently in Mardi Gras music such as Sugar Boy Crawford's "Jockomo" and other New Orleans-style tunes like Little Richard's "Slippin' and Slidin'" (1956).

Two-measure riffs were much more common, the most prominent being variants on the *transposable* "boogie-woogie" bass used by pianists since the 1930s. These lines more or less outlined triads and seventh chords, climbing up through the chord, reaching an apex on the downbeat of the second measure, then retrograding through the notes already played. Such bass lines, with their steady slow-wave motion, appeared in countless rhythm and blues and rock 'n' roll recordings of the 1950s. But two-measure riffs that did not simply outline seventh chords also appeared. Two of the most influential two-measure *non-transposable* riffs were those in Howlin' Wolf's "Smokestack Lightnin'" (1956) and Dale Hawkins's "Suzie Q" (1957). Both riffs imitated the descending melodic lines that often characterized rhythm and blues vocal melodies—beginning high, explosively, then falling in register and intensity.

Influenced by these and other riff-based songs, rock 'n' roll groups devised countless two-measure transposable riffs to fit their standard twelve-bar blues progressions. In the late 1950s and early 1960s such riffs appeared occasionally in soul recordings, but much more frequently in rock 'n' roll instrumentals. The instrumental groups of the early 1960s created many a "new" song by simply making up a riff and transposing it to the various levels of a twelve-bar blues progression.

British rhythm-and-blues oriented groups, however, returned to *two-measure non-transposable* riffs. The Yardbirds covered "Smokestack Lightnin'" and the Rolling Stones covered "Suzie Q," but both groups tended to lessen the riffs' technical demands: the Yardbirds played Howlin' Wolf's riff only occasionally in their rendition of the song; the Stones played Hawkins's original riff only occasionally, sometimes substituting a simpler, one-measure riff. These British groups also made their own *two-measure non-transposable* riffs, as in the Stones' hits "The Last Time" (1965) and "Satisfaction" (1965)—the latter a contrapuntally conceived riff, designed for bass and guitar playing interdependent lines.

Like their British precursors, American garage bands tended to favor *two-measure non-transposable riffs.* Pitch-wise, these riffs typically begin on the tonic, move to the subtonic or subdominant level (or both) at their mid-point, then back. Rhythmically, they begin with a strong downbeat (or perhaps two beats), grow slightly more complicated, perhaps via syncopation, then return to the beat at the end. Consider two characteristic examples. The Chocolate Watchband's two-measure "Are You Gonna Be There?" riff exhibits the typical rise and fall of pitch from tonic to subdominant, coupled with the increase and decrease of rhythmic complexity. The riff to Paul Revere and the Raiders' "Louie, Go Home" behaves similarly, but imitates the contrapuntal style of "Satisfaction."

49. On the background of this rhythmic riff see Jim Dawson and Steve Propes, *What Was the First Rock'n'Roll Record?* (Boston: Faber, 1992), 177–78; King Cotton, Notes to *Bo Diddley Beats* (Rhino Records CD R2 70291); Palmer, *Rock & Roll,* 69.

50. They may have been influenced in this regard by Wayne Fontana and the Mindbenders, who used the riff only in the *bridge* to their number one hit "Game of Love" (1965).

51. See Jim Dawson, "Louie Louie," *Discoveries* 61 (June 1993): 18–19.

52. The same riff appeared in an instrumental break in the Rolling Stones' cover of Dale Hawkins' "Suzie Q" (1964).

53. *Rolling Stone* dubbed it a "frenzied Xerox-Yardbirds raveup" while the *Rolling Stone Illustrated History of Rock and Roll* calls it the "all-time slopbucket copy of the Yardbirds." Actually some groups copied the Yardbirds' version of "I'm a Man," rave-up and all—see, for example, the Litter's cover.

54. Quoted in Jeremy Pascall, *The Rolling Stones* (London: Hamlyn, 1977), 76.

Chapter 4: The Not-So-Average "Joe"

1. Lester Bangs, *Psychotic Reactions and Carburetor Dung* (New York: Vintage, 1988), 8.

2. Marsh, *Heart of Rock & Soul,* 335.

3. Irwin and Fred Silber, *Folksinger's Workbook* (New York: Oak Publishers, 1973), 204.

4. This song appears in many sources, including John A. Lomax and Alan Lomax, *American Ballads and Folk Songs* (New York: Macmillan, 1951), 320–22.

5. Ibid., 557–60.

6. Ibid., 93–99.

7. Silber, *Folksinger's Workbook,* 223. See also the variants in Vance Randolph, *Ozark Folksongs,* 4 vols. (Columbia: Missouri State Historical Society, 1946) 1:67–71.

8. I am including those songs whose titles may include extra words, e.g., "Hey Joe, Bartender Joe" (1949). All of the copyright information contained herein comes from the United States *Catalogue of Copyright Entries* for the respective years.

9. The quotations are from Notes to *Frankie Laine: 16 Most Requested Songs* (Columbia Legacy cassette 45029).

10. Text taken from the copyright deposit EU 702387, 12 January 1962, words and music by William Roberts. The "or: smack through the head" is part of the original manuscript. (Some normalization of punctuation and spelling has been added.)

11. Martin Cohen, telephone conversation with the author, 26 July 1993. According to June Johnson, writing on behalf of Roberts in a letter to me dated 27 August 1997, Roberts "does not remember ever telling this story or anything close to it."

12. This claim comes from an anonymous e-mail source recounting a dialogue with Gary Duncan, a friend of the late Dino Valenti. The transcript, in my possession, was provided to me by Neal Skok.

13. Happy Traum, quoted in Robbie Woliver, *Hoot: A Twenty-five Year History of the Greenwich Village Music Scene* (New York: St. Martin's, 1986), 47.

14. Geoffrey Stokes, quoted in Woliver, *Hoot!*, 61.

15. Russell and Tyson, *And Then I Wrote*, 3.

16. Quoted in Woliver, *Hoot!*, 47.

17. Roberts via June Johnson, letter to the author, 27 August 1997.

18. The information and chronology concerning Valenti (often spelled "Valente") and Crosby derive from four sources: Ben-Fong Torres, "Dino Valente," *Rolling Stone* 26 (1 February 1969): 22–23; Steve Lake, "Dino: Trials and Tribulations," *Melody Maker* 49 (7 September 1974): 53; David Crosby and Carl Gottlieb, *Long Time Gone: The Autobiography of David Crosby* (New York: Doubleday, 1988), 67–68; and Valenti's obituary, *San Francisco Chronicle*, 18 November 1994.

19. The information in this and the following paragraph derives from interview comments by John Beck included in Ray Brandes, "The Leaves," *Ugly Things* 2 (1983, no page numbers); "The 'Hey Joe' File," *Byrds Flyte Chronicles* 8 (4th Quarter, 1987): 5–6; comments on the song by Dave Tulloch in the fanzine *A Letter from Home* 6, excerpted in *The Castle: The Love Connection* 3 (1994): 81; Charles P. Lamey, "The Leaves and The Merry-Go-Round: The Bill Rinehart Story," *Blitz* 49 (May–June 1984): 10–11; Neal Skok, telephone conversation with the author, 9 October 1993.

20. In this version, the group shouts the words "Hey Joe!" at the beginning of the pertinent verses, the first two chord cycles of the instrumental break, and the last three chord cycles of the song. After the lines about Joe's destination, the group plays three more chord cycles, then stops. Throughout, the lead singer uses speech-song to deliver most lines. Although the key is the same as Roberts's original, the singer changes the notes of the four-note melodic descent: instead of descending stepwise from A to E, he descends from F to C♯ (F-E-D-C♯). This latter change is uncharacteristic of later recordings of "Hey Joe"; but the speech-song is typical.

21. De Shannon's producer, Jack Nitzsche, takes credit for this riff. See Ken Barnes, "The Arranger as Superman: A Nitzschean View of Pop History," *Bomp* 16 (Winter 1976–77): 28.

22. The quote is from a recorded interview with members of the Leaves (Panda Records PAPD-1003).

23. A few lines vary from the earlier recording: Joe says he is going to "find" his woman, then, to the second question says he is going to "shoot" his woman, and then "shoot them both before I'm through." But the final verse more or less follows Roberts's original wording: Joe is going to "my place in Mexico . . . where a man can be free / There ain't gonna be no hangman puttin' no noose around me."

24. Some sources claim that the Leaves actually recorded the song another time between the first recording and this one, but never released it; I have even received a purported dub of this so-called second version (the hit version being the "third"). But I have found no corroborating evidence that the purported interim version was made; the dub I received was actually a dub of the first version.

25. They lengthen this standard eight-measure progression, however, to twelve measures, by extending the dominant chord for four more measures, which grow in intensity almost like a rave-up.

26. It spent nine weeks on the charts, peaking at number 31.

27. The Enemies' version also restored the melody to its original skeletal descent (A-G-F♯-E).

28. See Neal Skok's interview with Maclean in Vorda, *Psychedelic Psounds,* 137.

29. This also done for one cycle only in the version by the Stillroven.

30. The latter two recordings remained unreleased until compact disc compilations of the respective groups.

31. The group was Baronen.

32. The Golden Cups also changed the music. In the middle of the recording, the group plays a free-form psychedelic jam; throughout the recording, the bassist plays florid oriental riffs beneath the tonic chord.

33. Greg Shaw, Letter to the Editor, *Goldmine,* 8 April 1988.

34. Martin Cohen, telephone conversation, 26 July 1993.

35. M. Ross, "Tim Rose: More Than a Schmuck," *Rolling Stone* 111 (22 June 1972): 16.

36. He also could and did deliver the melody differently from most West-Coast groups. Rose's four-note melodic skeleton ends a third above the final chord instead of a fifth—but Rose then skips down to the root of the final chord: C-B-A-G♯-*E.* The transposition lowers the tune and, in the process, makes it more menacing. The addition of the root of the final chord of the cycle gives the tonic a greater weight than it had had before. Coincidentally, Rose's four-note skeleton is a transposed version of the Surfaris' (who do not add the final tonic that Rose does).

37. The latter recording credited the song to "Bryant Boudleaux," a garbling of the name of the author of Carl Smith's hit "Hey Joe!"

38. See the discussion of Hendrix and "Hey Joe" in John McDermott et al., *Jimi Hendrix Sessions: The Complete Studio Recording Sessions, 1963-1970* (Boston: Little, Brown and Co., 1995), 8-10.

39. Jimi Hendrix, quoted in Chris Welch, "Who Says Jimi Hendrix Can't Sing?" *Melody Maker,* 15 April 1967, p. 3.

40. After Rose, long ponderous versions abounded—at least one (by the Velvet Hammer) spanning both the A and B sides of a single.

41. Sean Bonniwell, telephone conversation with the author, 3 April 1998. Bonniwell is writing an autobiographical book tentatively titled *Beyond the Garage* (Porterville, Calif.: Christian Vision Publishing, forthcoming).

42. This attempt to show "Hey Joe" in two different incarnations resembles the recording of the song by the Soulbenders. In their version of the song, they start slowly and sing the Hendrix text up through the words "I caught her messin'

around town." Then they abruptly change to the Leaves style, beginning the text all over again and proceeding through a thoroughgoing cover of the Leaves, including the surf-music bridge.

43. The song may be heard on the compact disc *Pebbles,* vol. 4 (East Side Digital, ESD 80372).

44. Meanwhile neo-garage bands routinely cover the song, groups such as the Paisley Zipper Band, who in 1993(?) faithfully recreated the Leaves' version.

Chapter 5: Getting Psyched

1. For a good discussion of this aspect of psychedelic experience, see R. A. Durr, *Poetic Vision and the Psychedelic Experience* (Syracuse: Syracuse University Press, 1970), 53–55.

2. The quotes come from Albert Hofmann, *LSD: My Problem Child,* trans. Jonathan Ott (New York: McGraw-Hill, 1980), 17–19.

3. Roy F. Baumeister, "Acid Rock: A Critical Reappraisal and Psychological Commentary," *Journal of Psychoactive Drugs* 16 (October–December 1984): 344.

4. Richard Middleton and J. Muncie, "Pop Culture, Pop Music and Post-War Youth: Counter-Cultures," *Popular Culture* (Milton Keynes, England: Open University Press, 1981), 87, as quoted in Sheila Whiteley, *The Space Between the Notes: Rock and the Counter-Culture* (London: Routledge, 1991), 4.

5. Quoted in Jas Obrecht, "Turn On, Turn Up, Trip Out: The Rise and Fall of San Francisco Psychedelia," *Guitar Player* 326 (February 1997): 71.

6. Graham Nash, quoted in Chris Welch and Bob Dawbarn, "Psychedelic: The New 'In' Word," *Melody Maker* 41 (22 October 1966): 10.

7. Mickey Hart, in Michael Goldberg, "The San Francisco Sound," *Rolling Stone* 585 (23 August 1990): 96.

8. "The Curious Story behind the New Cary Grant," *Look* 23 (1 September 1959): 50–58.

9. Quoted in William Braden, "LSD and the Press," in Bernard Aaronson and Humphry Osmond, eds., *Psychedelics: The Uses and Implications of Hallucinogenic Drugs* (Garden City, N.Y.: Doubleday, 1970), 403.

10. The books are Constance A. Newland, *Myself and I* (New York: Signet, 1963), and Jane Dunlap, *Exploring Inner Space* (New York: Harcourt Brace and World, 1961).

11. My thanks to Robert J. Dalley for helping me ascertain the date and authors of this tune.

12. See Ed Ward, Notes to *The Holy Modal Rounders: Stampfel and Weber* (Fantasy Records 24711).

13. See the *New York Times,* 14 June 1966, 44:1.

14. Tom Wolfe, *The Electric Kool-Aid Acid Test* (New York: Bantam, 1969), 209. My thanks to Fay Kesey (telephone conversation, 14 April 1995) for her explanation of the thunder machines.

15. The advertising for the Trips Festival is reproduced in Paul D. Grushkin, *The Art of Rock: Posters from Presley to Punk* (New York: Artabras, 1987), 115–16.

16. Notes to *The Psychedelic Sounds of the 13th Floor Elevators* (International Artists IALP1).

17. Quoted in Leonard Wolf, *Voices from the Love Generation* (Boston: Little, Brown & Co., 1968), xxxiii–iv.

18. He had copyrighted the folk-oriented "Get Together" in 1963. It became popular in the San Francisco hippie context via cover versions by Jefferson Airplane (1966) and especially by the Youngbloods—led by former Greenwich Village folk singer Jesse Colin Young—whose 1967 recording of the song became a Top 10 hit in 1969.

19. Coltrane named his second son Ravi, after his friend and former teacher. Shankar also taught sitar to George Harrison of the Beatles. In 1967 he appeared at the Monterey Pop Festival—which through the D. A. Pennebaker film *Monterey Pop* (1968) represented West-Coast psychedelia to the whole nation. In 1969 Shankar appeared at Woodstock.

20. For the quote and further discussion of Coltrane's use of LSD, see Eric Nisenson, *Ascension: John Coltrane and His Quest* (New York: St. Martin's Press, 1993), 167.

21. See John Densmore, *Riders on the Storm: My Life with Jim Morrison and the Doors* (New York: Delacorte, 1990), 195.

22. In "India," the four-note riff is played in relative isolation by two saxophones; in "Eight Miles High" it appears at the beginning of the song and twice later, always as the opening of a twelve-string lead guitar solo—itself clearly derived from Coltrane's style. See Palmer, *Rock & Roll,* 164–65, for more on Coltrane's influence on rock in this period.

23. Quoted in Obrecht, "Turn On, Turn Up, Trip Out," 75.

24. Darby Slick, *Don't You Want Somebody to Love: Reflections on the San Francisco Sound* (Berkeley: SLG Books, 1991), 12.

25. See the comments of Paul McCartney in Mark Lewisohn, *The Beatles Recording Sessions: The Official Abbey Road Studio Session Notes, 1962–1970* (New York: Harmony Books, 1988), 14–15.

26. This paragraph derives from the information and quotations in Chris Welch and Nick Jones, "Who's Psychedelic Now?" *Melody Maker* 42 (14 January 1967): 9. In the quotation from the Move, the blanks appeared in the original, presumably because the journal refused to print "dirty" words.

27. The song's author, John Lennon, always insisted that the title came serendipitously from his son Julian's drawing of Lucy O'Donnell, a pre-school classmate. Julian described the picture as "Lucy, in the sky with diamonds." The picture is reprinted (along with a discussion of the song title) in Steve Turner, *A Hard Day's Write: The Stories behind Every Beatles Song* (New York: HarperCollins, 1994), 123.

28. See "Beatle Paul and LSD: Was He Right to Own Up?" *Melody Maker,* 1 July 1967.

29. As quoted in a retrospective in *Melody Maker,* 30 May 1987.

30. Alan Walsh, "The George Harrison Interview," *Melody Maker,* 2 September 1967, 8–9.

31. Billy James, quoted in Joe X. Price, "Music's Psychedelic Sound," *Variety,* 5 April 1967.

32. John Blofeld, "A High Yogic Experience Achieved with Mescaline," *Psychedelic Review* 7 (1966): 29. See also David Drake, "Psychedelic Metaphysics," *Psychedelic Review* 5 (1965): 56–57.

33. Timothy Leary, "The Experiential Typewriter," *Psychedelic Review* 7 (1966): 80. See also David E. Smith, "Lysergic Acid Diethylamide: An Historical Perspective," *Journal of Psychedelic Drugs* 1 (Summer 1967): 2.

34. Timothy Leary, "The Religious Experience: Its Production and Interpretation," *Journal of Psychedelic Drugs* 1 (Winter 1967–68): 10.

35. Quoted in Sculatti and Seay, *San Francisco Nights*, 84.

36. Quoted in ibid., 42, emphasis mine. See also p. 79 of the same source, where Peter Albin of Big Brother and the Holding Company recalls: "We were never really into jazz. We *thought* we were, but we could never play a single jazz lick." Ron Nagle of the early psychedelic group Mystery Trend explained: "None of us could really jam. . . . That was something jazz musicians did. They were articulate on their instruments. We were incapable of doing that" (ibid., 75).

37. Jim McCarty, interview with Mike Ober, http://www.idsonline.com/yardbirds.

38. Erik Braunn, quoted in "Iron Butterfly: Flight of the Phoenix," *Goldmine* 421 (13 September 1996), 26. Jerry Garcia gives another reason for the lengthening of songs: "We played long songs because people wanted to dance. That's what it was all about" (Sculatti and Seay, *San Francisco Nights*, 73).

39. The definition comes from Kramer, *Time of Music*, 7 and 50.

40. Quoted in Goldberg, "San Francisco Sound," 96.

41. My thanks to Steven Johnson for providing this term.

42. Quoted in Darby Slick, *Don't You Want Somebody to Love*, 80.

43. Jerry Richardson, "Who Am I, and So What If I Am?" in Aaronson and Osmond, *Psychedelics*, 53.

44. Whiteley, *Space Between the Notes*, 26.

45. Gregory Bateson, "Group Interchange," in Harold A. Abramson, ed., *The Use of LSD in Psychotherapy* (New York: Josiah Macy Jr. Foundation, 1960), 188.

46. On the use of reverberation in surf music, see Robert J. Dalley, *Surfin' Guitars: Instrumental Surf Bands of the Sixties* (N.p.: Surf Publications, 1988), 7–8.

47. A Native American informant quoted in Abraham Cáceres D., "*In Xochitl, In Cuicatl:* Hallucinogens and Music in Mesoamerican Amerindian Thought" (Ph.D. diss., Indiana University, 1984), 331.

48. Sculatti and Seay, *San Francisco Nights*, 110, call "Section 43" one of "the few recordings of the era that might legitimately be termed 'psychedelic.'" The Fish constructed other songs similarly, such as "Rock and Soul Music" (1968), a single song comprising three smaller songs.

49. The more obscure recordings to which I refer are: Teddy and his Patches, "Suzy Creamcheese"; Bohemian Vendetta, "Enough"; Opal Butterfly, "My Gration Or?"; and the Bougalieu, "Let's Do Wrong"; all of these are from ca. 1967. Promotional copies of the Buckinghams' "Susan" came with the collage edited out.

50. A prototypical rock example is "The Witch" (1964) by the Sonics. This is based on a twelve-bar blues progression, but adds to the second half of each measure a chord a half-step above each chord of the blues progression, in order to create a deviant, "occult" sound. Although not a "psychedelic" record—it deals with human evil, not the dementia of drugs—it suggests some of the technique of psychedelic music, how one could unnerve the harmony with simple half-step inflections.

51. This type of motion is extremely rare in rock 'n' roll. The only instance of which I am aware is the obscure single by Tony Shepperd, "Zack" (ca. 1960?), whose harmonic oscillation is identical to that of "House at Pooneil Corners." ("Zack" appears on the compact disc *Desperate Rock'n'Roll, Vol. 1,* Flame CD 001).

52. The chord progression, used repeatedly in the verse to this latter song, is [i | v ♭II | i].

53. Quoted in Obrecht, "Turn On, Turn Up, Trip Out," 76.

54. The historical information here comes from Obrecht, "Effects on Records," 25–26. For a discussion of Turner's use of the whammy bar see Palmer, "Church of the Sonic Guitar," 671–72.

55. Two of the best-known examples of these downward/upward chordal glissandi appear in the Ventures' hits "Walk Don't Run" (0:40 and 1:41) and "Perfidia" (0:17, 0:43, etc.), both recorded in 1960.

56. See "Michael Bloomfield Reminisces," *Guitar Player* 9 (September 1975): 16.

57. This is the assertion of Ray Manzarek, as conveyed to me by Kerry Humpherys.

58. A good summary of Bailey's "double-tonic complex" appears in Christopher Orlo Lewis, *Tonal Coherence in Mahler's Ninth Symphony* (Ann Arbor: UMI Research Press, 1984), 4–5.

59. Flamenco guitarists often use progressions of major chords built on E, F, and G.

60. Kantner, interviewed in Simon Albury and John Sheppard, producers, "It Was Twenty Years Ago Today," Granada TV, 1987.

61. Sculatti and Seay, *San Francisco Nights,* 21.

62. This situation should not be confused with "cross harp" playing in the blues, where the player uses a harmonica pitched a perfect fourth above the real key, in order to get the minor seventh.

63. Hendrix, quoted in *Melody Maker,* 30 May 1987, 14.

64. Timothy Leary, "The Second Fine Art: Neo-Symbolic Communication of Experience," *Psychedelic Review* 8 (1966): 10–11.

65. Obrecht, "Effects on Records," 28.

66. Hendrix, quoted in Jann Wenner and Baron Wolman, "It's Jimi Hendrix," *Rolling Stone* 1 (9 March 1968): 12. Hendrix apparently heard the wah-wah pedal in "Tales of Brave Ulysses"; see Art Thompson, "Burning the Midnight Amp: A Journey through 11 Years of Hendrix Gear," *Guitar Player* 309 (September 1995): 93.

67. Sculatti and Seay, *San Francisco Nights,* 171. This technique probably derives from similar techniques among jazz singers such as Sarah Vaughan and Nancy Wilson.

68. Lewisohn, *Recording Sessions,* 72.

69. Ibid., 50.

70. Consider Jefferson Airplane, "The Ballad of Your & Me & Pooneil" (1967), and Steppenwolf, "Magic Carpet Ride" (1968)—the latter of which includes fuzztone with the feedback.

71. For a brief but insightful discussion of Hendrix's use of feedback, see "Michael Bloomfield Reminisces," 36.

72. Lewisohn, *Recording Sessions*, 74. John Lennon always claimed he discovered the technique inadvertently while stoned and trying to thread a demo tape of "Rain" (1966). After "Rain," the Beatles routinely asked to hear their music backwards to see if any of it might be usable on record.

73. "Four Psilocybin Experiences," *Psychedelic Review* 1 (1963): 234.

74. The songs to which I refer are "Omaha" (1967) and "Just Dropped In" (1968), respectively.

75. See Ribowsky, *He's a Rebel*, 120.

76. In order to create the sound of a unison duo, ADT sent a recorded signal through a second recorder and superimposed the dub onto the original at a minutely different speed. George Martin had jokingly told Lennon that the technical term for this was "flanging"; the facetious term has since become standard.

77. See Lewisohn, *Recording Sessions*, 123.

78. As with "The Big Hurt," two mono tracks were superimposed in an attempt to simulate stereo. See the comments of vocalist Kenn Ellner in Devorah and Steve Hill, "Count Five," *Discoveries* 77 (October 1994): 53.

79. Eddie Kramer, "My Hendrix Experience," *EQ* 3 (October 1992): 76.

80. Hendrix interviewed by Jay Ruby (originally for *Jazz & Pop* magazine), reprinted in *Guitar World* 12 (November 1991): 45.

81. Notes to Eddie Wayne and Group, *The Ping Pong Sound of Guitars in Percussion* (Coronet Records CXS).

82. From an advertisement on the back of Ray Martin and His Orchestra, *Dynamica* (RCA LSA 2237).

83. Teresa Murphy, quoted in Wolf, *Voices from the Love Generation*, 196.

84. See Palmer, *Rock & Roll*, 172–73, for a good assessment of the lasting influence of psychedelic music.

Chapter 6: Playing with "Fire"

1. See Densmore, *Riders on the Storm*, 116 and 166–67; and James Riordan and Jerry Prochnicky, *Break on Through: The Life and Death of Jim Morrison* (New York: William Morrow, 1991), 149. Francis Ford Coppola had the character Kurtz teach the song to his soldiers in the film *Apocalypse Now* (the scene was edited from the final version)—see Dylan Jones, *Jim Morrison: Dark Star* (New York: Viking, 1991).

2. It is deemed a "standard" in Charlie Gillett, *The Sound of the City: The Rise of Rock and Roll*, rev. ed. (New York: Pantheon, 1983), 347; and Irwin Stambler, *Encyclopedia of Pop, Rock & Soul* (New York: St. Martin's Press, 1977), 167. *Rolling Stone*, 8 September 1988, 110, lists it in its survey of "The Best 100 Singles Ever Made." The "anthem" comment is from Lester Bangs, in Miller, ed., *Rolling Stone Illustrated History*, 280.

3. The recordings of "Light My Fire" to which I refer are only those made of the original Doors at the following shows: the Matrix, San Francisco, 10 March 1967; the Kaiserdome, San Bernadino, 4 July 1967; Denver, September 1967; the Ed Sullivan Show (CBS), 17 September 1967; Danbury High School (Connecticut), 17 October 1967; Winterland, San Francisco, 26 and 28 December 1967; the Jonathan

Winters Show (CBS), 27 December 1967; Back Bay Theatre, Boston, 17 March 1968; Hollywood Bowl, 5 July 1968; Singer Bowl, New York City, 2 August 1968; Chalk Farm Roundhouse, London, 7 September 1968; Amsterdam, 12 September 1968 (without Morrison); Kongresshalle, Frankfurt, 14 September 1968; Stockholm, 20 September 1968 (two shows); Chicago, November 1968; Forum, Los Angeles, 14 December 1968; Dinner Key Auditorium, Miami, 1 March 1969; Varsity Stadium, Toronto, 13 September 1969; Felt Forum, New York City, 17 and 18 January 1970; Long Beach Arena, 7 February 1970; N. E. Coliseum, Vancouver, 6 June 1970; and Isle of Wight Pop Festival, 29 August 1970. Many of these recordings have been issued commercially in the United States and Europe on compact discs, vinyl, videotapes, etc. Some exist only on audiotape; others have appeared on ephemeral, unlicensed non-commercial issues. The legal status of many of them remains unclear.

4. The date of the request comes from Densmore, *Riders on the Storm*, 61. Tim Bradley, "Robby Krieger," *Guitar World* 4 (January 1983): 42, quotes Krieger as saying that keyboardist Ray Manzarek requested the new songs. In all other sources I have been able to locate, however, Krieger and his bandmates attribute the request to Morrison. Riordan and Prochnicky, *Break on Through*, 113, probably base their statement that Manzarek requested the songs on Bradley's article. On the authorship and elemental imagery, see especially the interview with Krieger on KROQ radio, March 1991 (precise date unknown), cassette transcription in my possession. In this source, Krieger reports that these two songs, "Light My Fire" and "Love Me Two Times," were only the second and third he had ever written; also, Krieger's comments quoted in "The 100 Best Singles Ever Made," 110. According to Densmore (61), it was Morrison who told them to "use universal imagery instead of specifics. . . . earth, air, fire, [and] water." At the press conference following the Doors' induction into the Rock and Roll Hall of Fame, 13 January 1993, however, Densmore asked Krieger if Morrison hadn't suggested the four elements theme. Krieger laughed and said, "Somebody made that up, I think" (videotape in my possession).

5. Densmore recalls that the second verse lacked a second line: "The time to hesitate is through / Try now we could only lose / And our love become a funeral pyre." Morrison offered the line "No time to wallow in the mire," which Krieger accepted (see Densmore, *Riders on the Storm*, 64). That one line, however, was apparently the only one that producer Paul Rothchild thought was weak (see Riordan and Prochnicky, *Break on Through*, 271).

6. The original version of the song may be heard in the recreation of its origins depicted in Oliver Stone's 1991 movie *The Doors*: Krieger was the source for the musical details in that scene.

7. He played it with only two fingers of his left hand, giving only the pitches A, B, and E. The chord may be heard most clearly in live performances, especially from the Matrix, 10 March 1967; Krieger talks about his fingerpicking in Jas Obrecht, "Beyond the Doors: Robby Krieger," *Guitar Player* 17 (February 1983): 56.

8. As interviewed in a *Classic Cuts* radio segment, [summer?] 1987, cassette dub in my possession.

9. Densmore, *Riders on the Storm*, 62.

10. See Manzarek's discussion of this in the radio program *In the Studio/The Doors* (Bullet Productions, Burbank, California, 1991). In this source, Manzarek recalls always interpreting the A chord as A minor that way: "Robby starts to play the song . . . and [we] said, 'Hey, those are great chord changes'—A minor to F-sharp minor."

11. Manzarek has given many accounts of his composition of the introduction. Here I have relied on his statements in Riordan and Prochnicky, *Break on Through,* 112; *Classic Cuts;* and an interview in 1992 on WNEW radio (New York, cassette dub in my possession). This last source has come to be known as the "8-13-67" show, because the interviewer and interviewee act as if the show were being taped on that date, speaking of everything from that time in the present tense.

12. Manzarek in *In the Studio/The Doors.* Densmore discusses his attachment to Coltrane and Elvin Jones in Riordan and Prochnicky, *Break on Through,* 80; he specifically links "Light My Fire" to their version of "My Favorite Things" in *Riders on the Storm,* 195; also, in ibid., 67, he recalls that "the long, jazzy instrumental solos in 'Light My Fire' . . . were born at the [London] Fog," the club where the band played its first stint of performances.

13. The quotation is from Paul Rothchild, interviewed on the radio show *Off the Record,* 18 March 1991, Westwood One Productions. In this source Rothchild also sings the original melody and confirms the accuracy of the movie scenario in Oliver Stone's *The Doors.*

14. Quoted in Riordan and Prochnicky, *Break on Through,* 90.

15. The first eight measures of the solo form a small A-A^1 structure; the next four measures a B-B^1; the next two measures a C-C^1; and so forth. (The solo is transcribed in Robert L. Doerschuk, "Ray Manzarek of The Doors: Waiting for the Nubians," *Keyboard* 17, no. 2 [February 1991], on pp. 82–83.) We should note that Manzarek had to play the solo only with his right hand. He had to use his left hand to play the Fender keyboard bass, using a left-hand ostinato technique he had perfected through years of playing boogie-woogie—see Steven Rosen, "Ray Manzarek: From 'The Doors' to 'Nite City,'" *Contemporary Keyboard* 3 (September 1977): 44.

16. Krieger remarks on his solo in Bruce Pollock, "After the Fire," *Guitar* 5 (September 1988), 28.

17. The contrapuntal duo and retransition are easy to overlook in the studio recording. Most listeners perceive the solo section in two main parts, dominated by organ and guitar, respectively, and both of roughly equal lengths. Manzarek himself routinely describes the solo section as an organ solo followed by a guitar solo; the recording mix reinforces this interpretation, highlighting organ first, then guitar. Even though the contrapuntal duo emerges almost seamlessly from the guitar solo, as does the retransition from the duo, live performances clarified the four-part division. In some cases, as we will see, they divided the solo section even further.

18. The story is told in Densmore, *Riders on the Storm,* 103–4.

19. Ray Manzarek in *In the Studio/The Doors.*

20. Quoted in Riordan and Prochnicky, *Break on Through,* 141. For an appreciation of the solos' integral part in the song, see Doug Sundling and Diana Maniak, *The Doors: Their Artistic Vision* (Bluffton, Ind.: Greenfire! Publishing, 1990), 29.

21. Geoffrey Stokes in Ed Ward et al., *Rock of Ages: The Rolling Stone History of Rock and Roll* (Englewood Cliffs, N.J.: Rolling Stone/Prentice-Hall, 1986), 368–69.

22. The show was Winters's debut, airing on 27 December 1967, while the Doors were playing at Winterland. The group actually placed a television on the stage in order to watch their broadcast performance during their live show. For a fairly detailed reminiscence, see Densmore, *Riders on the Storm,* 156–58.

23. Unfortunately, this treatment obliterated one of the few harmonic connections in the song: whereas the E major chord that ended the chorus had served as a dominant to the A minor chord of the verse, it now was effectively neutralized by the G major chord that began the bridge.

24. See Densmore, *Riders on the Storm,* 174.

25. The "sample" in Example 5 is a partial transcription of the responsorial passage in their performance at Amsterdam, 12 September 1968. The organ pitches during those moments when the snare is sounding, however, were particularly difficult to transcribe, since the tape to which I had access lacks fidelity and balance.

26. Densmore, *Riders on the Storm,* 143. The long solo ostinato to which I refer is from the performance at Kongresshalle, Frankfurt, 14 September 1968.

27. Occasionally they played even fewer; but twelve seemed to become the standard.

28. Densmore, *Riders on the Storm,* 194–95.

29. In Doerschuk, "Ray Manzarek," 88.

30. Jones, *Dark Star,* 104.

31. Meltzer, *Aesthetics of Rock,* 155—a comment that is amplified later in the book (216).

32. Densmore, *Riders on the Storm,* 70, reports on a particular occasion at the London Fog in early 1966. During the solo section, Densmore recalls, Morrison began sticking a strong-smelling capsule of amyl nitrites under the noses of the players: "I tried to squirm away without getting up or stopping the song. . . . Robby, being mobile with his guitar cord, got away. . . . As Ray swayed back and forth, trying to avoid [it], his hands flailed wildly at the organ and the tempo of 'Light My Fire' sped up deliriously."

33. Quoted in Riordan and Prochnicky, *Break on Through,* 267.

34. See Harvey Parr, "At the Hollywood Bowl," *Los Angeles Free Press,* 15 July 1968; and Densmore, *Riders on the Storm,* 170.

35. Interviewed in Paul Williams, *Outlaw Blues: A Book of Rock Music* (New York: Dutton, 1969), 112.

36. Incidentally, the published version of the song never changed. It remained true to the original recording's melody, including the dissonant D against the harmonic C♯.

37. Doerschuk, "Ray Manzarek," 90.

38. In Densmore's opinion, the Buick offer brought to a head the tensions in the group; some associates trace the Doors' eventual breakup to this episode. This incident has been treated on many occasions: see Riordan and Prochnicky, *Break on Through,* 270–71; Densmore, *Riders on the Storm,* 202–3; and Frank Lisciandro's radio program *The Doors: Three Hours for Magic* (Jon Sargent Productions, 1981).

39. Densmore, *Riders on the Storm*, 182.

40. As quoted in Edd Jeffords, "Doors at Seattle," *Poppin* [July 1969?], reprinted in Danny Sugerman, *The Doors: The Illustrated History*, ed. Benjamin Edmunds (New York: William Morrow, 1983), 149.

41. The tape shows that he yelled: "I wanna see some dancing, yeah I wanna see some fun, wanna see some dancing. There are no rules, there are no laws. Do whatever you wanna do! Do it! . . . Now listen, anybody who wants to come up here and join us and do some dancing, come on, just get on up here. Come on, come on."

42. An excerpt from the court transcript published in *The Doors Collectors Magazine* 6 (Spring 1995): 26.

43. James Spurlock, "Doors Play It Cool," *Chicago Daily News*, 16 June 1969, reports that the group played the song as an encore after *both* sets. Jeffords, "Doors at Seattle," complains about the group's lackluster performance of the song.

44. Riordan and Prochnicky, *Break on Through*, 330.

45. Quoted in ibid., 358.

46. To get a sense of this ambivalence, compare recordings of the song from the Felt Forum, New York, 17 and 18 January 1970 (early shows)—the former energetic and the latter completely disengaged.

47. They kept the original form of the song intact, except that, in at least one instance, they omitted the final reprise of Manzarek's organ introduction, ending instead with Morrison's high note on the word "fire," above a sustained tonic chord. This omission may have been provoked by Densmore's feeling that the organ introduction *as an ending* left the song sounding unresolved.

48. Jones, *Dark Star*, 52. On Presley's influence on Morrison, see the comments of Bruce Botnick quoted in Riordan and Prochnicky, *Break on Through*, 111. In his early Sun recordings, Presley mastered a peculiar shift between a frontal, grinding "head tone" suggestive of black gospel and a throaty, covered "chest tone" characteristic of white popular vocalists of the 1940s. (To hear the shift clearly, see his delivery of the chorus to "Good Rockin' Tonight": "I heard the news, there's good rockin' tonight".) Within a few years Presley moved his voice almost entirely into the throaty realm that became the staple of imitators, including Morrison.

49. The musical quotation of "When the Music's Over" was in the performance of "Light My Fire" at Long Beach, February 1970.

50. Vince Treanor describes the scene in Riordan and Prochnicky, *Break on Through*, 438.

51. According to Riordan and Prochnicky, *Break on Through*, 483.

52. Dan Hartman, "Relight My Fire" (Blue Sky Records JZ 36302). For a stereotypical disco version of "Light My Fire," see the album *Silver Blue* (Epic 35474).

Chapter 7: Ends and Means

1. Gary Burns, "A Typology of 'Hooks' in Popular Records," *Popular Music* 6 (January 1987): 16, suggests that certain endings involving interesting edits actually become the "hook" of the song, the chief attraction of the recording itself.

2. See Jim Dawson and Steve Propes, *What Was the First Rock'n'Roll Record?* (Boston: Faber, 1992), 3–4.

3. Ibid., 23.

4. Groups then reinherited the problem of how to end the same song live. At least one group used live fades for humorous effect—see Dan Hicks and the Hot Licks, "Traffic Jam," recorded live on *Where's the Money?* (1972, Blue Thumb BTS 29).

5. For a review of literature on the psychology of repetition and likeability, see Philip A. Russell, "Effects of Repetition on the Familiarity and Likeability of Popular Music Recordings," *Psychology of Music* 15 (1987): 187–97.

6. To be sure, some rock artists simply used studio technology to update the old way of ending with an embellished final chord. Some applied a rapid echo effect to the chord, a technique prevalent in recordings made around Los Angeles in the mid-1960s by many highly "produced" surf and post-surf pop groups—for example, the Ragamuffins' "The Fun We Had" (1966), the Lyrics' "Wake Up to My Voice" (1966), and even the Mothers of Invention's "Help, I'm a Rock" (from the album *Freak Out!* 1965). Such endings sounded modern enough, but contributed little to the ending as a structural component.

7. Producer George Martin explained: "I knew we needed a backwash, a general mush of sound, like if you go to a fairground . . . just a tremendous chaotic sound. So I got hold of old calliope tapes, playing 'Stars and Stripes Forever' and other Sousa marches, chopped the tapes up into small sections and had Geoff Emerick throw them up in the air, re-assembling them at random." Finding that this "random" assemblage still sounded too orderly, Martin added that "we switched bits around and turned some upside down" (quoted in Lewisohn, *Recording Sessions,* 99). The two collages appear at 1:00–1:26 and 1:52–2:36.

8. A bootleg reproduction of the acetate appears on *The Beatles: Acetates* (Yellow Dog Compact Discs [Luxembourg] YD 009).

9. See ibid.

10. The evolution of the recording is detailed in Lewisohn, *Recording Sessions,* 94–99 passim.

11. See ibid., 128.

12. These begin, respectively, at 2:53 and 3:02.

13. At 3:14.

14. The quotation begins at 3:23. While Lennon sings in the same key as "All You Need Is Love," he metrically displaces the fragment of "She Loves You," placing the first "yeah" (and not "loves") on the downbeat. The general effect was more important than the specific quotation in John's mind: in rehearsal, he had sung "Yesterday" and even "She'll Be Coming Round the Mountain" (see Lewisohn, *Recording Sessions,* 120).

15. Steve Race of the BBC, transcribed on the Beatles, *Unsurpassed Masters, Vol. 3* (Yellow Dog compact disc YD003).

16. From 2:44–3:12.

17. Jon Lomberg, "The Tripping Eye," in Lester Grinspoon and James B. Bakalar, eds., *Psychedelic Reflections* (New York: Human Sciences Press, 1983), 88.

18. Examples of momentum introduced at the end of the song (when energy seemingly needs to be dispersed) would include the Crystals' "He's a Rebel" (1962);

at the end, in gospel fashion, the meter changes to double-time—only to fade quickly.

19. This is a fine instance of what William Fowler describes as Hendrix's "onomatopoeic" guitar playing—quoted in Bill Milkowski, "Jimi the Composer," *Guitar World* 9, no. 2 (March 1988): 163–64. While most delaminations use instruments only, the one found in Paul Revere and the Raiders' "I Don't Know" (1969) is primarily vocal. From 3:20 to 4:05 the rhythm section fades, while the voices (with slight accompaniment by organ and lead guitar) remain until 5:33.

20. It is perhaps fair to mention the similar effect at the end of Haydn's "Farewell" Symphony, in which the various instruments drop out one by one until only two violins remain to play the closing measures.

21. See Janet Schmalfeldt, "Cadential Processes: The Evaded Cadence and the 'One More Time' Technique," *Journal of Musicological Research* 12 (1992): 1–52.

22. In their hit cover version of the song (1964), the Dave Clark Five did not use the technique.

23. The track time on compact discs of this recording is given as 3:55, suggesting that the first fade is considered the real ending, while the final seconds of fade-in material is gratuitous.

24. This resumption occurs only in the stereo mix of the song. The mono mix of the song omits the resumption altogether, fading out completely for the one and only time by 3:36. See Lewisohn, *Recording Sessions,* 154.

25. Its persistent rapid tom-toms derive from both Buddy Holly's "Peggy Sue" (1957) and the Surfaris' "Wipe Out" (1963).

26. This is available on *The Beatles: Unsurpassed Masters, Vol. 3.* The Beatles deleted this substitution for the final recording.

27. This ending may be heard on *The Beatles: Unsurpassed Demos* (Yellow Dog compact disc YD 008).

28. See Lewisohn, *Recording Sessions,* 155. Tim Riley (*Tell Me Why: A Beatles Commentary* [New York: Knopf, 1988], 285) calls this a "haunting outtake . . . wedged in between 'Cry Baby Cry' and 'Revolution No. 9.'" Yet the track divisions on the album show that it is not "between" the two but attached to the first.

29. See Sergei Eisenstein, *Film Form* (New York: Meridian Books, 1957), 37–40.

30. Riley, *Tell Me Why,* 211.

31. The Grateful Dead, Quicksilver Messenger Service, and the Mothers of Invention all exemplified this technique.

32. Quoted in Lewisohn, *Recording Sessions,* 191.

33. Riley, *Tell Me Why,* 324.

34. The story is told in detail in Lewisohn, *Recording Sessions,* 183.

Appendix 1: Sources

1. Gunther Schuller deals with a similar issue in his *Early Jazz: Its Roots and Musical Development* (Oxford: Oxford University Press, 1968), x.

2. David Brackett discusses this whole issue in his *Interpreting Popular Music* (Cambridge: Cambridge University Press, 1995), 27–29.

3. See the fine discussion of recordings as works of art and varying formats in Gracyk, *Rhythm and Noise*, 22-31.

4. Lenny Kaye, quoted in the retrospective on *Nuggets: Original Artyfacts from the First Psychedelic Era, 1965-1968,* in *Rolling Stone* 507 (27 August 1987): 160.

5. David Walters, *The Children of Nuggets: The Definitive Guide to 'Psychedelic Sixties' Punk Rock on Compilation Albums* (Ann Arbor: Popular Culture, Ink., 1990).

6. Quoted on the back jacket of Clinton Heylin, *Bootleg: The Secret History of the Other Recording Industry* (New York: St. Martin's Griffin, 1996).

7. Ibid., 3.

8. Herbert I. London, *Closing the Circle: A Cultural History of the Rock Revolution* (Chicago: Nelson-Hall, 1984), v-vi.

9. Robert Patison, *The Triumph of Vulgarity: Rock Music in the Mirror of Romanticism* (New York: Oxford, 1987), viii.

10. James F. Harris, *Philosophy at 33⅓ rpm: Themes of Classic Rock Music* (Chicago: Open Court, 1993), xiii.

11. Susan McClary and Robert Walser, "Start Making Sense: Musicology Wrestles with Rock," in Simon Frith and Andrew Goodwin, eds., *On Record: Rock, Pop, and the Written Word* (New York: Pantheon, 1990), 285.

12. Quoted in Bill Flanagan, *Written in My Soul* (Chicago: Contemporary Books, 1987), 343.

13. In Barthes, *The Responsibility of Forms: Critical Essays on Music, Art, and Representation,* trans. Richard Howard (New York: Hill and Wang, 1985), 267-77. The scholars of whom I speak are Simon Frith, *Sound Effects: Youth, Leisure, and the Politics of Rock* (London: Constable, 1983), 164-65; McClary and Walser, "Start Making Sense," 282; George Lipsitz, "Against the Wind: Dialogic Aspects of Rock and Roll," *NARAS Journal* (Spring 1992): 8-9; Dave Laing, *One Chord Wonders,* 54-55.

14. Ironically, none of the aforementioned rock scholars cites Barthes's actual example of such an analysis, in a lecture entitled "Music, Voice, Language." There Barthes lists five phonetic features of his beloved Panzéra's voice—how he forms and projects characteristic vowels and consonants—as well as timbre, resonance, and, above all, the states of character that these vocal traits seem to signify (Barthes, *Responsibility of Forms,* 278-85).

15. Frith, *Sound Effects,* 164.

16. From an interview conducted by Hector Bianciotti, 1973, in Roland Barthes, *The Grain of the Voice: Interviews 1962-1980,* trans. Linda Coverdale (New York: Hill and Wang, 1985), 184.

17. Frith, *Sound Effects,* 165. Frith's comment also implicitly detaches Presley's "grain" from all others. But consider, for example, the lead vocal of the Eagles' original Mercury recording of "Trying to Get to You" (1954), which Presley later covered. Few listeners would be capable of distinguishing it from Presley, who clearly used it as a model for his vocal style.

18. Moore, *Rock, the Primary Text,* 43.

19. Charlie Hodge, quoted in "Elvis Presley: An Oral Biography," *Musician* 168 (October 1992): 59.

20. In Presley's case, how could one hear the contrasting personae? To begin with, note how in his earliest recordings he sings high notes frontally—"in the

mask," as vocal pedagogues would say—and lower notes in the throat, with a dark, covered sound. He is able to move suddenly and dramatically between these two modes of vocal projection. In the process he maintains an aesthetic tension that he then intensifies by frequent glottal stops, and by chopping phrases, sub-phrases, and even single words into short bursts of sound, momentarily transforming the voice into a percussion instrument. The frontal sound and glottal stopping clearly derive from country singing tradition, but the covered sound from some of the more polished forms of rhythm and blues singing, from crooners, and, above all, from singers such as Mario Lanza—whom Presley claimed was his greatest influence as a singer. See the comments in Patsy Guy Hammontree, *Elvis Presley: A Bio-Bibliography* (Westport, Conn.: Greenwood Press, 1985), 40, 154.

To appreciate Presley's synthesis of implied personae (and its dynamic aesthetic), one need only listen to Roy Brown's original recording of "Good Rockin' Tonight" (1948) and Junior Parker's original of "Mystery Train" (1953), then compare Presley's cover versions, both recorded in his 1954 sessions with Sun Records. Whereas Brown and Parker both project a smooth, continuous, covered vocal sound, Presley fluctuates between that sound and his frontal country voice, adding short bursts of vocal percussion. Presley's vastly accelerated tempos enhance the excitement, projecting, in place of Brown and Parker's cool detachment and control, an unmistakable abandon and enthusiasm—an energy conveyed no longer by power but by sheer speed. And that was an important transformation if one was to create a distinctly youthful music. Regrettably, soon after his Sun sessions Presley began singing in a continuously covered way (e.g., in "It's Now or Never," 1960). This technique dominated most of his later recordings and tended to legitimize him among some "trained" musicians.

21. Walser, *Running with the Devil: Power, Gender, and Madness in Heavy Metal Music* (Hanover, N.H.: Wesleyan University Press, 1993), 42. See also the discussion of "noise" as an aesthetic category in Gracyk, *Rhythm and Noise*, 99–124.

22. See Blecha, Notes to *Nuggets; Volume Eight: The Northwest,* and the particularly rabid polemic on this theme in Rev. and Mrs. Tommy Parasite [*sic*], "The Boy Looked at Roky," Part 2, published as Notes to Vol. 8 of *Pebbles: Original Artyfacts from the First Punk Era* (BFD Records 5025).

23. "The Boy Looked at Roky." Adding insult to injury, this writer adds: "The best thing to come out of England in the late 60's was Jimi Hendrix, an American Negro from Seattle who wasn't good enough to play in any of the local bands like the Sonics or Paul Revere & the Raiders."

24. William Ruhlmann, Notes to *The Legend of Paul Revere* (Columbia CD 45311), 5.

25. Don Waller, Notes to *Nuggets; Volume One: The Hits* (Rhino Records RNLP 025).

26. Bangs, "Protopunk," 261.

27. See Laing, *One Chord Wonders,* 149, n. 17. Indeed, in one of the earliest treatments of this music Lenny Kaye called it "punk," although scholars have abandoned that term for American garage bands of the 1960s and applied it to the musical and cultural phenomenon of the 1970s and 1980s.

28. He mentions only a vague sonorous affinity among Ritchie Valens's "La Bam-

ba" (1958), several mid-1960s recordings by the Kingsmen and the Kinks and later recordings by the Stooges and the Ramones. "There," he writes, one can hear "twenty years of rock & roll history in three chords, played more primitively each time they are recycled" (Bangs, "Protopunk," 261).

29. Dr. Weasel [sic], "That Grooving Garage Band Sound," *Cryptic Times* 1 (Fall 1990): 22.

30. Beverly Paterson, *Journey to the Center of the Garage: A Guide to Obscure American Psychedelic Punk Bands of the Sixties* (San Mateo, Calif.: Emerald Publications, 1990), 4.

31. Marsh, *Heart of Rock and Soul,* 57.

32. Whiteley, *The Space Between the Notes,* 4. Respecting this book, I more or less agree with the critical review of it by Matthew Brown, *Notes: Quarterly Journal of the Music Library Association* 50 (September 1991), 205.

33. There are precedents in Western music, works that associate drug effects and music: the *Symphonie Fantastique* of Berlioz, for example, and even works like J. S. Bach's "Coffee" cantata. But no other style of music in western history has been predicated on drug use.

Appendix 2: Names

1. In his study of 1970s punk, Dave Laing laid groundwork for the understanding of rock group names and the identities they project. In a brief survey, he considers several broad categories: "naturalistic" name formulae, i.e., the use of *family* names (The Jacksons) or *leader + followers* names (Gerry and the Pacemakers); names connoting musicality, wealth, or both; names referring to other phenomena in contemporary culture; and "non-sense" names (Laing, *One Chord Wonders,* 42–49). A very brief treatment of rock band names also appears in Frank Nuessel, *The Study of Names: A Guide to the Principles and Topics* (Westport, Conn.: Greenwood Press, 1992), 111. Robert Walser devotes a paragraph to heavy metal band names in his *Running with the Devil,* 2. Two large lists of names of mid-sixties San Francisco groups have been published: Bobby Abrams, "Buckskin Comes to the Haight," in Eisen, ed., *Age of Rock 2,* 235–37 (this also includes some groups from Iowa); and the more complete list in Ralph J. Gleason, *The Jefferson Airplane and the San Francisco Sound* (New York: Ballantine, 1969), 330–40. My own observations derive from combing through record catalogues, indices, advertisements, and so forth. I have been aided greatly in understanding *how* groups got their names by Adam Dolgins, *Rock Names* (New York: Citadel, 1993).

2. Dolgins, *Rock Names,* 153.

3. The Ravens claimed that their name came not from the bird, but from the fact that everyone was "raven" about their sound (Dolgins, *Rock Names,* 168).

4. The reference here is to Raleigh cigarettes, which had a coupon on the back of each pack.

5. Quoted in Frith, *Sound Effects,* 189–90.

6. Mick Jagger, quoted in Dalton, *Rolling Stones,* 13.

7. Frith, *Sound Effects,* 75.

8. Platt et al., *Yardbirds,* 21.

9. On the Drifters, see Dolgins, *Rock Names,* 72–73.

10. The quote here and comments from the group on the name are in Jon Savage, *The Kinks: The Official Biography* (London: Faber and Faber, 1984), 17; see also Ray Davies, *X-Ray: The Unauthorized Autobiography* (Woodstock, N.Y.: Overlook Press, 1995), 103.

11. Saxon, quoted in Vorda, *Psychedelic Psounds,* 174.

12. Dolgins, *Rock Names,* 38.

13. Ibid., 220.

14. The latter group recalls that they chose their name because "at the time insects were the big thing" (Dolgins, *Rock Names,* 110).

15. See Dolgins, *Rock Names,* 142, for more on the latter name.

16. Strawberry Alarm Clock cites Donovan's reference to "electrical banana" (in "Mellow Yellow," 1967) as an influence on this kind of name (Dolgins, *Rock Names,* 190–92).

17. Laing, *One Chord Wonders,* 44.

18. Poggioli, *Theory of the Avant Garde,* 37.

19. Notes to the Leaves, *Hey Joe* (Mira Records LPS 3005).

20. Dolgins, *Rock Names,* 34. A few groups were more calculating: Creedence Clearwater Revival, for example, spent "two weeks of concentrated effort" deciding on their name (Dolgins, *Rock Names,* 52).

21. Dolgins, *Rock Names,* 91.

22. Platt et al., *Yardbirds,* 21.

Index

Index of Song Titles

MICHAEL HICKS is a professor of composition and theory in the School of Music at Brigham Young University. He is the author of *Mormonism and Music: A History* and dozens of articles in journals, including *Musical Quarterly, Perspectives of New Music, Journal of the American Musicologial Society,* and *American Music.* He is also the coauthor, with Steven Johnson, of a forthcoming book on the composer Henry Cowell.

Music in American Life